I couldn't have done this project without the help of many good people. I dedicate this book to them, my heroes:

John Platt, always the motivator and positive thinker and all of his contributions on my behalf.

My wife Amy- For keeping me grounded and humbled and my three children for their support

My Mom for all the encouragement you have given me in the Kitchen, and being such a great test subject

RL (Dad) For being our cheerleader and coach.

Barbara Ferguson, for without her unrelenting persistence in connecting me with Smoke Alarm Media and helping me get this book done- Thank you, Thank you.

Thanks to my gang, the Blue Axe Crew- Matt, Dan, Chris, Ryan and Chris S. and Tanner

For all my family and friends who encouraged and even acted like they were interested

To my Sierra Trading Post Family, thank you for putting me in a position where I could show off my skills.

Camille Eide- My rock star of a sister who happens to be a novelist.

Bryan Wilkins- My sounding board and Test Chef

Sherri Aulbach- My consummate promoter

Emmy Smith- Photography of Primus Cooking Equipment

The Idahosummits Message Board as field test subjects on our outings.

Cooking in the Mountains Field Test Subjects: Dan Robbins, Dave Pahlas, John Platt, Margo Mandella, Margie Ankrum, Pat McGrane, Matt Eells, Dan Biddle, Ryan Porter, Chris Randolph, Chris Shippy, Tanner Weston and Slade Weston

A HUGE "Thank You" to both GSI and Primus, for making great cooking equipment and supporting me and In The Wild Chef book.

You can find us at www.InTheWildChef.com and on Facebook: In The Wild Chef

Photography by Stephen Weston and team, except where noted

Library of Congress Control Number: 2010914234

Weston, Stepehen

In The Wild Chef: Recipes From Base Camp to Summit

  ISBN 978-1-927458-06-8

Printed in the United States of America

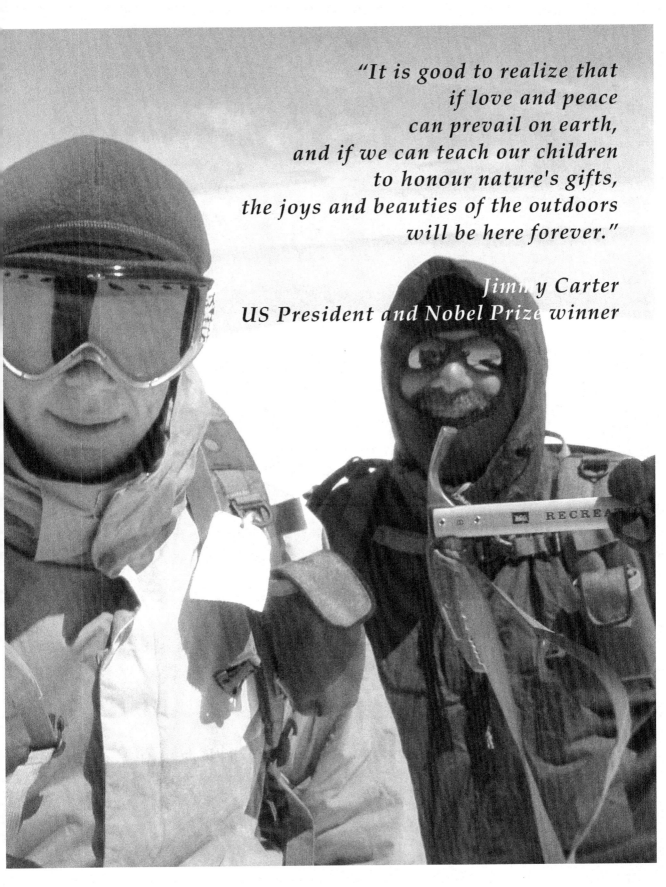

"It is good to realize that
if love and peace
can prevail on earth,
and if we can teach our children
to honour nature's gifts,
the joys and beauties of the outdoors
will be here forever."

Jimmy Carter
US President and Nobel Prize winner

BIG NASTY TRAIL
2 MI. SEMI-LOOP

it. Most charges end without injury.

IF A BEAR ATTACKS
Brown bear: Play dead unless it starts
to eat you, then fight back.
Black bear: Fight back.

Dragon's Mouth Spring
This spectacular belching action of turbid water from this underground cavern is due to escaping steam and sulfureous gases from beneath the bank. The sounds are due to the splash of water against the walls of hidden caverns. The temperature is 185°F and the heat comes from deep within the earth.

Now since this is a cookbook, I should have organized everything under its proper heading, like soups, pasta, desserts and the like. But instead, it is organized by the way we camp, by Classes

In The Wild Chef

The Hungry Backpacker by Ryan Porter...........................7

The Classes...

Many a hungry backpacker has arrived at camp to the dismal sight of an over-priced, freeze-dried meal..... and resolved immediately with intense conviction that the menu must be improved.

The outdoor experience provides a myriad of different satisfactions for participants, but there is a constant for us. If we are going to stay some duration in the wilderness, we must pack food with us (unless your friends will tolerate the sight of a llama's backside all the way up the trail) that means, your food is on your back. And so the great debate is born. How much weight should we be willing to pack to enrich our high-elevation cuisine? Has any subject been hashed out more than this one over the ol' campfire?

The weight vs. taste argument is one old and worthy. Multi- day backpacking circumstances demand that people reasonably determine whether he or she shall either consume dehydrated muck, or pay dearly through the quads, hamstrings, calves, etc., in order to dine well

Steve's Smoked Salmon Chowder, getting an extra helping of smoke.

Ryan Porter

A curious bear seeing what's going
on at Yosemite National Park

In The Wild *Chef*

in the mountains. The author is among those of us who found himself at this same perplexing crossroads only to discover and admit that he is simply a prisoner to his very distinguished taste buds. This crossroad became the embarking of his odyssey of research and experimentation toward the medium between weight and flavor.

Some damaged cartilage and a few backpacks later, Stephen Weston has been successful in finding a number of combinations that explode with flavor and they won't herniate you carrying to camp. (so successful, that some big name brands have paid him to come along on back-country ski filming excursions as a cook) His passion for simultaneously bagging peaks and eating like royalty outruns his logical ability to settle for one or the other- and our palates can be the beneficiaries of his efforts.

Friends and I have welcomed the sight of recipes prepared by the author on a snowy, windy slope or two. Especially that salmon dish! Weston has provided something wholesome to the people around him, and that's all any of us can try for. Eat well and climb high.

Ryan Porter

The Recipes...

Bacon and Cheese Pasta

Everything is good with Bacon on it, especially after a day of rafting in the Northwest.

3 oz package of Ramen Noodles (any flavor – save seasoning packet for use at another time)
or use baked ramen or chukka soba noodles
¼ C. shelf stable bacon
¼ C. shelf stable parmesan cheese
¼ tsp granulated, dried garlic
¼ tsp red pepper flakes
¼ tsp ground black pepper
1 Tbsp olive oil
1½ C. water

NOTE: olive oil packets can be found online through www.minimus.biz or www.packit-gourmet.com

dry weight 6 oz

AT HOME:
1. Combine bacon, cheese and seasonings in a snack size ziplock bag.
2. Tuck ramen and oil packet inside; seal.
[If doing the recipe freezer bag style, pack the ramen in a qt freezer bag.]

AT CAMP:
Freezer bag method
1. Bring water to a near boil and pour over ramen; seal tightly and put in a cozy for 5-10 minutes.
2. Drain off water; toss with oil and seasonings.

Insulated mug method
1. Break up Ramen; add to mug.
2. Add boiling water; cover tightly 5-10 minutes.
3. Drain off water and toss with oil and seasonings.

One pot method
1. Bring water to boil; add ramen.
2. Cook 3 minutes; drain water and toss with oil and seasonings.

Suitable pitch refers to a good campsite location, with good drainage.

Big Dan's Spicy Hummus

Bringing an international flavor to being In The Wild.
Idahosummits.com would be proud

CLASS 1

CLASS 2

CLASS 3

CLASS 4

CLASS 5

Ingredients	Instructions
2-12 oz cans of chickpeas 2 Tbsp olive oil 6 Tbsp sesame oil (tahini) 4 garlic cloves, minced 1 jalapeño (finely diced) 1 red bell pepper juice of three lemons 1 Tbsp cayenne powder or red pepper seeds	**AT HOME:** **1.** Devein and remove seeds of red pepper and jalapeño. **2.** Boil until tender. **3.** Remove skins and combine with chickpeas; mash with a fork. **4.** Add the olive oil, tahini, and cayenne or red pepper seeds and lemon juice [If the mix is too thick, add two Tbsp water]. **5.** Add the garlic; mix until smooth. **6.** Store in zip lock bag. **IN CAMP:** **1.** Serve with slices of pita bread, crackers or tortillas.

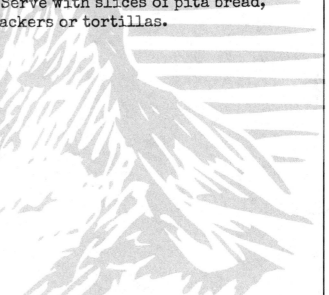

"Real freedom lies in wildness, not in civilization."
Charles Lindbergh

15

Bogus Basin Bakers

Throw on the grill or place in the coals of your fire.

4 medium potatoes
4 Tbsp butter, softened
4 Tbsp coarse salt
2 Tbsp garlic powder
1 Tbsp pepper
2 Tbsp Italian seasoning (optional)
4 squares of foil

AT HOME or AT CAMP:
1. Preheat an outdoor grill for medium-low heat.
2. Prepare four foil squares large enough to fold over one potato each.
3. Spread butter onto foil in large enough area so potatoes will be completely covered when foil is rolled.
4. Sprinkle with seasonings.
5. Roll each potato with foil.
6. Puncture package (including potato) with knife or fork a few times.
7. Grill for 1 hour or until soft, turning potatoes often.
8. Serve with your favorite toppings.

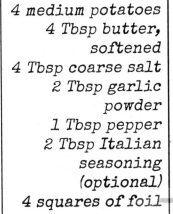

A south wind in the winter usually indicates a winter storm is approaching.

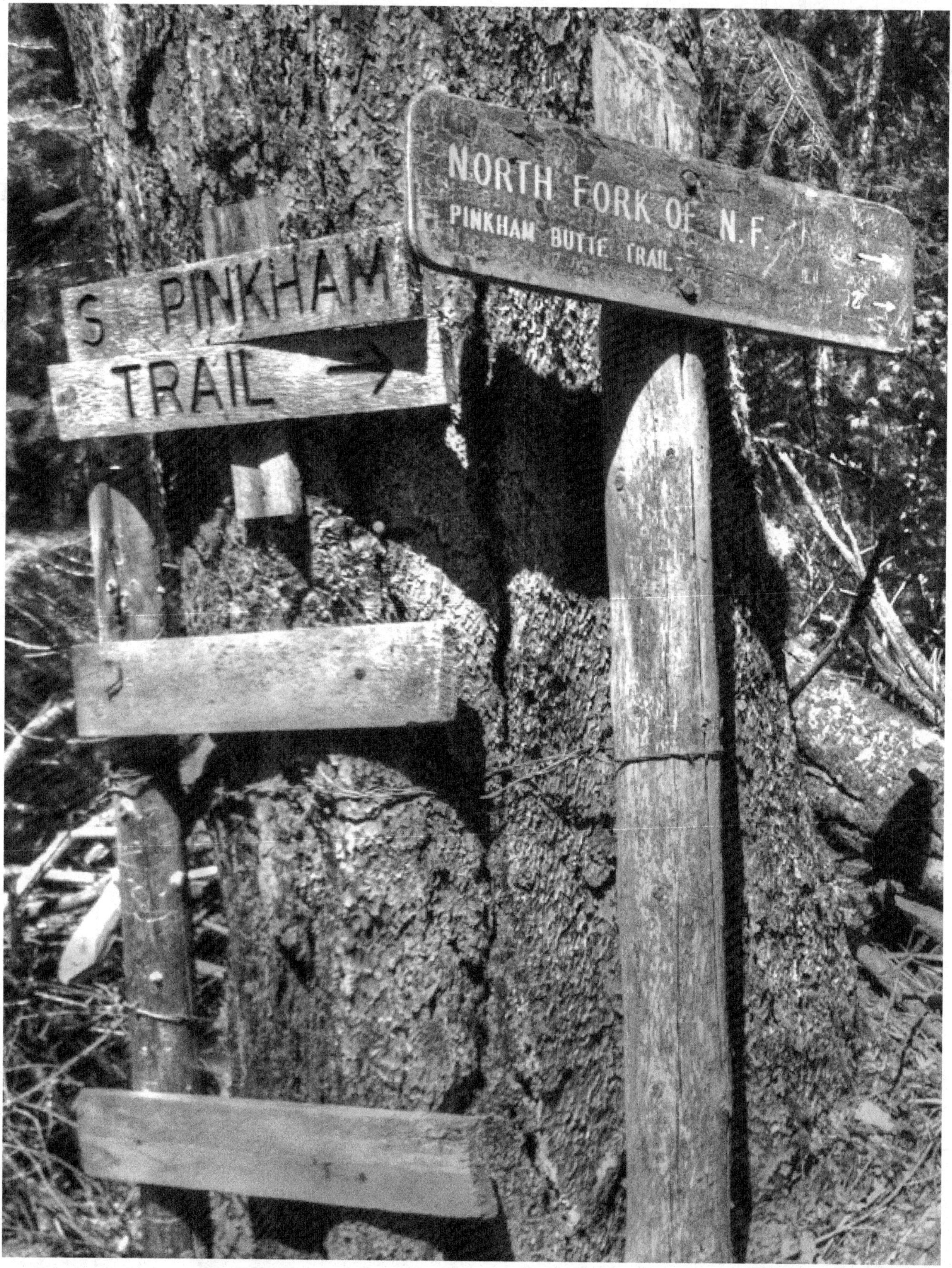
S PINKHAM
TRAIL
NORTH FORK OF N.F.
PINKHAM BUTTE TRAIL

Breakfast Quinoa

A healthy alternative to the standard oatmeal, and it has more protein. Always a plus.

1 C. water
⅓ C. instant Quinoa
1 tsp powdered milk
2 tsp brown sugar
½ tsp cinnamon
1 Tbsp ground flax seed
½ C. "Craisins"
¼ tsp nutmeg

At Home:
1. Combine all ingredients in a freezer bag for transport to camp.

At Camp:
1. Bring water to boil.

2. Add ingredients and continue to simmer for 90 seconds.

3. Serve and enjoy!

Feeds four hungry hikers.

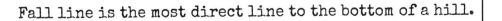

Fall line is the most direct line to the bottom of a hill.

Café Grafenwhor Mint Coffee

Bavaria's best!

¼ C. powdered creamer

⅓ C. sugar

¼ C. instant coffee

2 Tbsp powdered baking cocoa

2 hard candy peppermints

AT HOME:
1. Combine all ingredients and process in blender until well mixed.

2. Store in Ziploc baggie.

AT CAMP:
1. Place desired amount (approx. 1 Tbsp per cup of water) of mix into each mug; stir.

Noggin is a cup made from the burl of a tree.

20

Cappuccino Bars

No time to make coffee or fix breakfast— Just do this.

3 eggs
1¼ C. sugar
2 tsp vanilla
¼ C. butter, melted
2 C. all-purpose flour
½ tsp salt
¼ C. instant coffee crystals
¼ C. milk or heavy cream
1 C. pecans, chopped
½ C. mini chocolate chips

AT HOME:
1. Preheat oven to 325° F
2. Lightly grease a 13 x 9 " pan
3. Beat the eggs in a mixing bowl until light and fluffy
4. Add the sugar, vanilla and butter, beating to combine
5. Stir in the flour and salt (set aside 1-1/2 C. of batter.
6. Stir together coffee crystals and cream and add to the remaining batter
7. Spread the coffee batter into the prepared pan
8. Add chocolate chips to the reserved batter and spoon over the coffee batter
9. Run a knife through the two batters to marble them
10. Sprinkle the pecans over the top
11. Bake 20-25 minutes or until center is firm and set.
12. Cool before cutting into bars.
13. Wrap tightly in plastic wrap.

IN CAMP: Unwrap and enjoy!

Lofty cumulus clouds (cotton candy) usually indicate good weather.

Old cabin in the Sawtooth
Mountains, Idaho.

Chicken & Stuffing

This is one of the easiest recipes to prepare...and trust me, it's delicious! Call it Thanksgiving In A Box...

CLASS 1

1 - ½ C. water
¼ lb. butter or 4 Tbsp olive oil
1 - 6oz pkg. Stovetop stuffing mix
2 - 5 oz cans canned or foil pack chicken
½ C. chopped celery
½ C. "Craisins"

IN CAMP:
1. Boil water and stir in instant stuffing, chicken (the juice in the pouch too!), olive oil and celery.

3. Let rest for 2 minutes; stir in the Craisins.

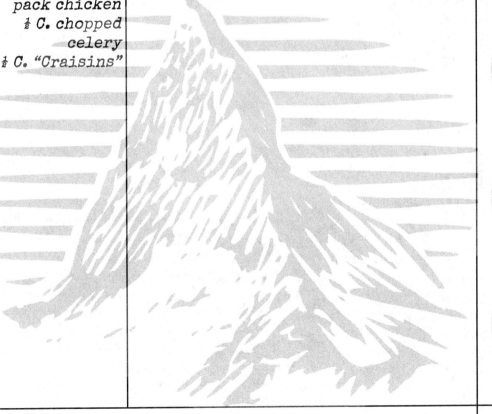

CLASS 2
CLASS 3
CLASS 4
CLASS 5

Some Simple Firestarters:
1. Take 100% cotton balls and thoroughly rub Vaseline into them.
2. Newspaper cut into strips. Roll up and tie with string. Cover with melted wax.
3. Use lint from your dryer as a fire starter.

Chicken Alfredo

What can we say about Chicken Alfredo? How about "Excuse me, garcon, but could you bring the wine now?"

2 C. water
1 pkg dry Alfredo spice mix
1 C. penne pasta
5 oz chicken breast (canned or foil pack)
3 Tbsp powdered milk

IN CAMP:

1. Bring water to a boil. Add pasta and cook for 5 minutes.

2. Add Alfredo mix and powdered milk.

3. Simmer for 8 minutes.

4. Add chicken and liquid from package.

5. Let stand until chicken has warmed through.

Serve and enjoy!

"I would feel more optimistic about a bright future for man if he spent less time proving that he can outwit Nature and more time tasting her sweetness and respecting her seniority."
E. B. White

Chicken Quinoa

Good for ya, fast and tasty.

½ C. quinoa

1 Tbsp dried chives

1 packet of True Lemon (or 1 tsp lemon juice or zest)

¼ tsp ground coriander

¼ tsp ground cumin

¼ tsp paprika

1 - 3 oz foil packet of chicken

1 C. water

AT HOME:

1. Combine everything except chicken in quart size Ziploc freezer bag.

2. Place chicken in separate bag.

AT CAMP:

1. Bring water to boil; add quinoa and spices.

2. Reduce heat and simmer 10-15 minutes or until water has been absorbed.

3. Add chicken.

4. Toss and serve.

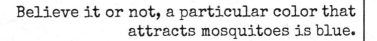
Believe it or not, a particular color that attracts mosquitoes is blue.

SENTIERO DEL
VIANDANTE
COMUNITA' MONTANA
VALSASSINA VALVARRONE
VAL D'ESINO RIVIERA

SENTIERO DEL
VIANDANTE
COMUNITA' MONTANA
VALSASSINA VALVARRONE
VAL D'ESINO RIVIERA

| Vezio | 0.15 |
| Varenna | 0.30 |

Regolo

Perledo | 0.15

0.15

Chicken Tetrazzini

Why deny yourself tastiness when you are on the trail?
Easy Italy in a pouch.

1 C. water

1 pkg mushroom soup mix

1 pkg ramen noodles

1 can chicken (5 oz)

AT HOME:
1. Mix dry ingredients except ramen and seasoning packet; store in sealable bag.

AT CAMP:
1. Boil water.

2. Add noodles and seasoning packet.

3. Stir in chicken.

4. Cook until noodles are tender.

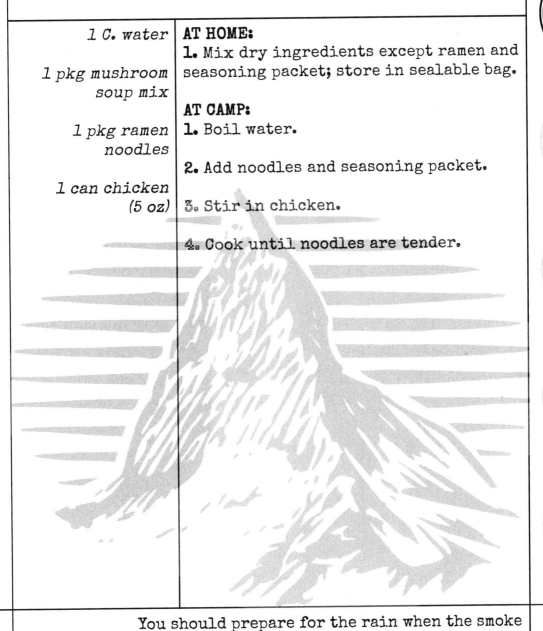

You should prepare for the rain when the smoke from your campfire hugs the ground.

Chocolate Mangos & Ginger

Island Paradise!

1 - 7 oz pkg
semi-sweet
baking chocolate

10 pieces
crystallized
ginger

10 slices dried
mangos

2 Tbsp peanut oil

AT HOME:
1. Pour peanut oil into small plastic bottle.

2. Place mango and ginger into Ziploc bag.

AT CAMP:
1. Fill a pan ¾ full with water; place on stove over medium heat.

2. Place chocolate in metal cup or small pot in pan (this prevents chocolate from burning).

3. Pour in peanut oil; stir until chocolate melts.

4. Dip each slice of mango and ginger into chocolate, eating as a fondue.

The "helve" of an axe is the handle.

Crab Chowder

Langoustinos are jealous.

CLASS
1

CLASS
2

CLASS
3

CLASS
4

CLASS
5

½ C. canned corn

½ C. imitation crab meat

1 C. cut vegetables: celery, onions, tomatoes, bell pepper or others of your choice

1 C. water

AT HOME:
1. Pack all ingredients into a 4" x 6" Ziploc bag.

AT CAMP:
1. Combine ingredients in pot with water; bring to boil and continue cooking for 1-2 minutes.

2. Remove pot from stove and place inside insulated cozy for 10 minutes.

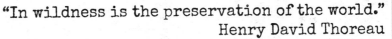

"In wildness is the preservation of the world."
Henry David Thoreau

Deano's Fried Apples

The biggest Peak bagger I know.

CLASS 1

5 apples peeled cored and sliced

¼ lb. butter (or oil)

1 tsp ground cinnamon

1 pinch salt

AT CAMP:

1. Melt oil or butter in medium sized fry pan over medium heat.

2. Add apple slices; cook slowly turning as slices begin to soften.

3. When fork tender, season with salt to taste.

CLASS 2
CLASS 3
CLASS 4
CLASS 5

Slant tube construction is the warmest sleeping bag construction.

Dried Beef Chowder

Lighting fast and easy.

CLASS 1

5 oz dried beef, shredded (optional: pepperoni, sausage crumbles or jerky in place of beef)
1 Tbsp butter
1 pkg Knorr ® potato with leek soup
3 C. water
¼ C. powdered milk

OPTION:
Replace leek soup with beef or vegetable soup mix
Add freeze dried vegetables

AT CAMP:
1. Mix all together and bring to a boil.

2. Simmer 5 minutes.

Cardinal points are found on a compass.

35

Ham and Pea Ramen

Childhood Favorite!

1 – 2 pkgs ramen noodles

½ C. dried peas

2 Tbsp parmesan

¼ C. ham, diced

Red pepper flakes (to taste)

2 C. water (use pkg instructions for amount)

AT HOME:
1. Repack ramen noodles and dried peas into one Ziploc bag (reserve flavor packets for later use in another recipe).

2. In another bag, combine cheese, ham and pepper.

AT CAMP:
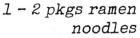
1. To a pot of boiling water, add first packet ingredients.

2. Once cooking, drain water.

3. Mix in second packet ingredients.

4. Simmer 3 minutes or until noodles are soft.

NOTE: if more of a soup consistency is desired, pour out only partial amount of water.

Air flow cushion is necessary around your camp stove because it keeps the fuel tank from overheating.

37

Johnny VooDoo Brownies

He was a child from the sixties.

Ingredients	Instructions
2¼ C. brown sugar tightly packed	**AT HOME:**
¾ C. unsalted butter (1½ sticks)	1. Preheat oven to 350.
2 Tbsp instant espresso	2. In a medium sauce pan combine brown sugar and butter over medium-low heat until butter is melted; remove from heat.
1 Tbsp hot water	3. Dissolve espresso powder in hot water and stir into the butter mixture.
2 eggs	4. Cool to room temperature.
2 Tbsp pure vanilla extract	5. Beat eggs and vanilla into cooled butter mixture.
2 C. flour	6. Sift together flour, baking powder and salt, stir into butter mixture.
2 tsp baking powder	7. Stir in the pecans, macadamia nuts and chocolate chips.
½ tsp salt	8. Grease 11 x 7 x2"baking pan9.
½ C. chopped pecans	9. Spread mixture evenly into prepared pan.
½ C. chopped macadamia nuts	10. Bake until lightly browned about 30 minutes.
1 C. semisweet chocolate chips	11. Cool and cut into squares.
	12. Place into container for the trail.

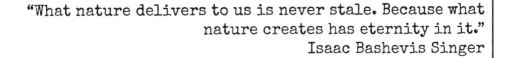

"What nature delivers to us is never stale. Because what nature creates has eternity in it."
Isaac Bashevis Singer

39

Margie's Mountain Granola

Mmm Mmm Good!

8 C. oatmeal
⅓ C. vegetable oil
⅓ C. brown sugar
1 C. honey
1 tsp pure
vanilla extract
½ tsp salt
½ tsp cinnamon
1¼ C. shelled,
unsalted
sunflower seeds
(toasted)
⅔ C. sesame seeds
(toasted)
1 C. sliced
unsalted almonds
(toasted)

1. Preheat oven to 350.
2. Place oatmeal in a large bowl.
3. In a medium sauce pan heat oil, brown sugar and honey over medium heat until thin (about 5 minutes).
4. Remove from heat.
5. Add vanilla, cinnamon and salt.
6. Pour over oatmeal.
7. Add sunflower seeds, sesame seeds and almonds and toss to combine.
8. Spread evenly on two baking sheets.
9. Bake 15 minutes stirring every 5 minutes.
10. Cool for a couple hours. (Don't eat it all....)
11. Put into 12 small sealable plastic bags (8 oz) for the trail.

Toasting Seeds:
1. Pre-Heat Oven to 350 degrees.
2. Place Seeds on baking sheet.
3. Bake for 10-15 minutes until toasty brown.

The bow of a canoe is located on the front.

Momo's Mexican Chicken and Rice

Loco Pollo!

1 C. instant rice

1 pkg tomato soup mix

½ tsp taco seasoning

1 can chicken (5 oz)

1½ C. water

AT HOME:
1. Mix dry ingredients; store in sealable bag.

AT CAMP:
1. Bring water to boil.
2. Add rice mixture.
3. Stir in chicken.

"Some national parks have long waiting lists for camping reservations. When you have to wait a year to sleep next to a tree, something is wrong."
George Carlin

'Nawlin's Black Beans

French Quarter Street Fare

Water	**AT CAMP:**
	1. Bring water to a boil.
1 pkg "Vigo" black beans and rice size	**2.** Add beans and rice package (despite package instructions, you will not need oil as the sausage will provide the needed grease.
1 lb Emeril Lagasse's "Kicked Up a Notch" smoked sausage (or other spicy sausage) cut into cubes	**3.** Per package instructions, boil for 1 minute, then simmer for additional 20.
	4. After first 15 minutes, add sausage and cook until rice is soft (may be additional minutes needed depending on altitude).

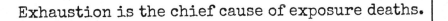

Exhaustion is the chief cause of exposure deaths.

Potato Pancakes

Hearty and filling.

½ C. add-water-only pancake mix

1¼ C. potato flakes

1 Tbsp granulated onion

AT HOME:
1. Combine dry ingredients and place into Ziploc bag.

AT CAMP:
1. Add just enough water to bag to make mixture into an easily handled dough.

2. Knead gently to form dough.

3. Form small balls and drop into lightly greased pan, smashing into patties.

4. Brown both sides.

"Queen Anne's lace" is another name for the wild carrot.

Rocky Road Pudding

After a day on the Rocky Trail.

1 – 3 oz box instant chocolate pudding

$\frac{2}{3}$ C. powdered milk

$\frac{1}{4}$ C. chopped pecans or walnuts

$\frac{1}{4}$ C. mini marshmallows

AT HOME:
1. Combine dry ingredients and place into Ziploc bag.

2. Carry nuts and marshmallows in separate bag.

AT CAMP:
1. In a bowl, add 2 C. water to dry ingredients.

2. Allow pudding to set.

3. Place in bowls or mugs and top with condiments.

Green is "zen." Research shows that first-hand experience with nature, like those at camp, reduce stress in children and help them better handle stress in the future.

Russian Tea

Warms you from the inside out.

1-12 oz package lemonade mix
1-18 oz jar "Tang" or orange powdered drink mix
1 C. sugar
1 tsp ground cloves
2 tsp cinnamon
2 tsp powdered ginger
½ C. candied "Red Hots"

1. Mix all together and keep in tight container until ready to use.

At Home or On the Trail:
1. Use 2 – 3 heaping tsp of tea mixture to a cup of hot water.

"In God's wildness lies the hope of the world – the great fresh unblighted, unredeemed wilderness. The galling harness of civilization drops off, and wounds heal ere we are aware."
John Muir

Salsa Chicken

You will make this at home when you taste how good this is.

CLASS 1

CLASS 2

CLASS 3

CLASS 4

CLASS 5

4 boneless, skinless chicken breast halves

1 jar salsa

Foil

AT HOME:
1. Place chicken in Ziploc bag.
2. Carry salsa separately.

AT CAMP:
1. Wrap each piece of chicken in a foil "envelope".
2. Pour salsa over chicken and wrap tightly.
3. Place over fire and cook for 40 minutes.

NOTE:
If you don't have a grill over the fire, place on a rock near the fire but not directly in the flames and cook for same amount of time, turning every 10 – 15 minutes.

Camp is a great place to try new activities and hobbies.

Sawtooth Sean
Survival Cookies

My best effort for my favorite Mountaineer.

1 C. softened butter or margarine
1 C. brown sugar
1 C. granulated sugar
2 eggs
1 tsp vanilla extract
2 C. flour
1 tsp baking soda
½ tsp baking powder
½ tsp salt
3 C. rolled oats
2 C. corn flakes
2 C. puffed wheat
1 C. dried, shredded coconut or sunflower kernels

AT HOME:
1. Preheat oven to 400 degrees and lightly coat 2-3 baking sheets with non-stick cooking spray.
2. In large mixing bowl, cream together margarine and sugars.
3. Beat in eggs and vanilla.
4. In separate bowl sift, flour, baking soda, baking powder and salt and gradually stir these into sugar mixture.
5. In large roasting pan or bowl, combine remaining ingredients.
6. Pour dough mixture over and mix by hand.
7. Drop by tablespoon onto baking sheets.
8. Bake 8- 10 minutest or until golden.

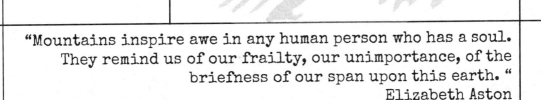

"Mountains inspire awe in any human person who has a soul. They remind us of our frailty, our unimportance, of the briefness of our span upon this earth. "
Elizabeth Aston

T Mo Caramel Apple

Back to Jackson we go!

1 single serving
pouch hot apple
cider mix

2 oz butterscotch
schnapps

AT HOME:
1. Pack schnapps into leakproof container and place in Ziploc bag with pouch of cider.

AT CAMP:
1. Boil water.

2. Make cider according to package instructions.

3. Add liquor.

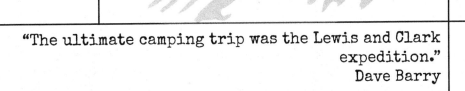

"The ultimate camping trip was the Lewis and Clark expedition."
Dave Barry

53

Alpine Lake Pasta

An easy mountain lake meal that could be paired with fish!

Ingredients	Instructions
2 - 4.4 oz Knorr butter & herb pasta packets	**AT HOME:** 1. Put tomatoes into sealable bag. 2. Store pasta and other ingredients in separate bag.
4 oz pepper-coated salami	**AT CAMP:** 1. Bring water to boil; pour over tomatoes.
2 oz sun-dried, diced tomatoes	
6 green onions, chopped	2. In separate pot, cook pasta according to directions.
5 oz gruyére cheese	3. Chop softened tomatoes.
1 C. water	4. After pasta cooks 5 minutes, add all ingredients and stir until noodles are done.

Camping has played an important role in the lives of some of the most talented people in history..Teddy Roosevelt, Henry Ford, Thomas Edison and Ernest Hemingway.

Bella's Beefy Noodle Bowl

Get out those Chopsticks and enjoy!

3 Tbsp beef jerky,
shredded
1 – 3 oz pkg Ramen
noodles
1 – 1 oz pkg
instant onion
soup
2 Tbsp dried
mixed vegetables
¼ tsp garlic
powder
¼ tsp ground
ginger
½ tsp dried
cilantro
1 – 2 packets soy
sauce

AT HOME:

1. Combine dry ingredients in quart size freezer Ziploc bag, saving flavor packet for later use.

AT CAMP:

1. Boil water; add to Ziploc.

2. Stir well until noodles are soft and vegetables rehydrated.

3. Season with soy sauce to taste.

Research shows that participation in intentional programs, like camp, during summer months helps stem summer learning loss.

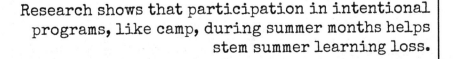

Boise Chowder

Soon to be a Idaho classic.

1 C. dried instant hash browns
¼ C. diced dried onions
4 tsp low sodium vegetable or beef bouillon
1 tsp dried parsley
¼ tsp diced dried garlic
¼ tsp dried thyme
¼ tsp ground black pepper
½ C. instant mashed potatoes
¼ C. shelf stable parmesan cheese
¼ C. fried onions
1 Tbsp olive oil (1 packet)
4 C. water

AT HOME:

1. Put hashbrowns and seasonings in ziploc bag.

2. Put instant potatoes, parmesan cheese and fried onions; tuck in oil. In a second ziploc bag.

AT CAMP:

1. Add hashbrown/seasoning bag and water to pot; cover and set aside 15 min.

2. Add oil; stir and bring to boil; lower heat and simmer 5 min.

3. Turn off stove and add contents of cheese/potato bag; stir well.

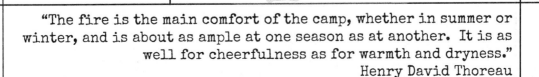

"The fire is the main comfort of the camp, whether in summer or winter, and is about as ample at one season as at another. It is as well for cheerfulness as for warmth and dryness."
Henry David Thoreau

Breakfast Scramble

You are tired, throw it in the boiling water and eat it out of the bag.

3½ C. instant mashed potatoes

1 C. freeze-dried eggs (w/ bacon optional)

3 C. water

2 Tbsp powdered milk

Cheddar Cheese (optional)

AT HOME:
1. Combine all dry ingredients and place into zip lock freezer bag.

2. If using cheese, add to separate bag.

IN CAMP:
1. Heat water in pot; bring to a boil.

2. Add ingredients in freezer bag.

3. Let sit 5 minutes.

4. Top with cheese.

Breakfast is the most important meal on the trail. It provides the majority of energy for the day.

Campfire Popcorn

Listen to it, when it stops, its done. I didn't know bears liked popcorn!

Popping corn

Oil

18" x 18" heavy duty foil squares

Butter and salt to taste

NOTE:
Use 1 tsp popping corn with 1 tsp oil per packet

AT CAMP:

1. Place oil in center of foil.

2. Add popcorn.

3. Seal edges by folding, tenting to allow room for the popcorn to pop.

4. Tie each pouch to a long stick with a string.

5. Hold pouch over hot coals or stove, or skillet and shake constantly until all kernels have popped.

6. Season with butter and salt.

"Even in a time of elephantine vanity and greed, one never has to look far to see the campfires of gentle people."
Garrison Keillor

Cheesy Bacon Mashers

Goes well with ANYTHING, especially a steak.

1¼ C. instant mashed potatoes

⅓ C. powdered milk

3 Tbsp cheese powder (or 1 Tbsp cubed cheddar)

¼ tsp ground black pepper

3 Tbsp shelf stable bacon or bacon bits

2¼ C. water

Note:
Cheese powder can be found in bulk food sections of grocery stores, online or from pkg of macaroni and cheese.

AT HOME:
1. Pack everything except bacon into a quart freezer or sandwich bag.

2. Pack bacon in separate bag.

AT CAMP:
Freezer Bag Method
1. Add near boiling water to bacon and all other ingredients to bag.

2. Stir well and let cool.

Dew appears when the atmosphere is dry.

Chelsea's
Chicken and Dumplings

She will fight you for the lumps.

2¼ C. water

1 pkg Ramen chicken noodles

1 – 5 oz can (or foil pack) chicken breast

¼ C. powdered milk

¼ C. Bisquick powdered milk

IN CAMP:

1. For dumplings: combine Bisquick and milk in a small baggie.

2. Add ¼ C water and knead until dough forms.

3. Boil remaining water and add noodles and chicken.

4. Simmer 3 minutes while adding penny sized pieces of dumpling mix into soup.

5. When dumplings are done, remove from heat and serve.

In fair weather, air currents drift up hillsides in the afternoon.

Creamy Rosa Chicken Pasta

Easy gourmet after a long hike.

8 oz small shaped pasta
1 C. freeze dried chicken
$\frac{1}{2}$ C. diced sun-dried tomatoes
$\frac{1}{4}$ C. freeze dried bell pepper
$\frac{1}{4}$ C. freeze dried celery
1 Tbsp diced dried onion
1 Tbsp diced dried spinach
$\frac{1}{3}$ C. powdered milk
1 (1.3 oz) packet Knorr Parma Rosa sauce mix
1 Tbsp olive oil (1 packet)
4 Tbsp shelf stable parmesan cheese
4 C. water

NOTE:
You may substitute 1-7 oz canned chicken

AT HOME:
1. Pack pasta, chicken and vegetables in quart ziplock bag.

2. Place milk and sauce mix into snack size bag;; tuck in the cheese and the oil packets.

AT CAMP:
1. Boil water; add pasta bag and return to boil.

2. Lower heat to simmer and cook until desired doneness.

3. Remove from heat and stir in oil and dry sauce mix.

4. Stir well; let meld 1-2 minutes then stir in cheese.

Toque is a Canadian word for a knit stocking cap.

Curried Rice

Change it up, life's too short.

CLASS 1

CLASS 2

CLASS 3

CLASS 4

CLASS 5

1 C. instant rice
½ Tbsp curry powder
1 Tbsp dried onion flakes
¼ tsp sugar
½ Tbsp chicken or vegetable bouillon
¼ tsp garlic powder
⅛ tsp ground turmeric
Salt and pepper to taste
1 C. water

OPTIONAL:
Chopped cashews to top
Foil packet chicken

AT HOME:
1. Combine all ingredients in quarter freezer Ziploc bag.

2. If bringing chicken, carry separately.

AT CAMP:
1. Bring water to boil; add to rice mix.

2. Steam inside bag for 1-2 minutes or until rice is tender.

3. Add chicken (optional).

4. Top with chopped cashews (optional).

Frostbite is directly related to wind-chill. It's more important to be out of the wind.

Gordy's Gorp Balls

Gordy likes easy, this is easy.

$\frac{1}{3}$ C. each:
raisins, apples,
apricots, dates
and coconut

$\frac{1}{2}$ C. sesame seeds

$\frac{1}{3}$ C. walnuts

2 C. peanuts

1 C. chocolate
chips

$\frac{1}{3}$ C. honey

$\frac{1}{2}$ C. peanut butter

AT HOME:

1. Mix chocolate, honey and peanut butter.

2. Add other ingredients.

3. Shape into balls.

A "baffled foot" can be found on a sleeping bag.

Grilled Peaches

A way to a girls heart.

	AT CAMP:
1-½ Tbsp butter	**1.** Melt butter in skillet.
3 Tbsp brown sugar	**2.** Stir in brown sugar and rum.
⅓ C. rum (preferably dark rum)	**3.** Stir until sugar dissolves.
	4. Place peach halves in large bowl.
8 ripe peaches – peeled, pitted and halved	**5.** Pour butter/rum mixture over and stir gently to coat.
	6. Grill over medium heat, about 5 minutes per side, brushing with left-over butter mixture as they grill.

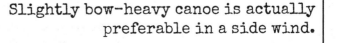
Slightly bow-heavy canoe is actually preferable in a side wind.

Ham and Cheese Macaroni

Just like Mom's, out of a box.

¼ C. deli ham, dried

¼ C. mixed vegetables, dried (corn, carrots, peas and green beans)

½ C. macaroni

1 Tbsp + 1 tsp cheddar cheese powder

1 Tbsp powdered milk

1 C. water

AT HOME:

1. Combine ham, vegetables and macaroni in a quart ziploc bag.

2. Combine cheese and milk powders in a ziploc bag; enclose in larger bag with other ingredients.

AT CAMP:

1. Add water and large bag of ingredients in water to hydrate 5 minutes.

2. Bring water to boil, cover and continue cooking on medium to high heat for 2 minutes.

3. Quickly stir in small bag ingredients; replace lid.

4. Place pot into insulated cozy for 10 minutes for meal to continue to hydrate and cook.

"There is a solitude, or perhaps a solemnity, in the few hours that precede the dawn of day which is unlike that of any others in the twenty-four, and which I cannot explain or account for."
George Bird Grinnell

Banana Smoothie

Refreshing and fun, reward yourself.

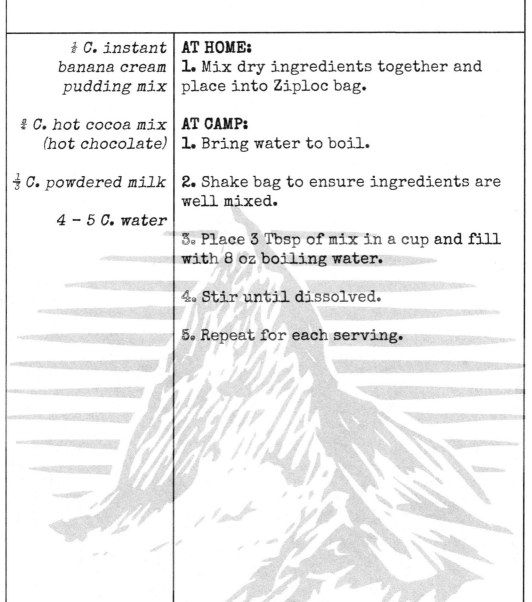

¼ C. instant banana cream pudding mix	**AT HOME:** 1. Mix dry ingredients together and place into Ziploc bag.
¾ C. hot cocoa mix (hot chocolate)	**AT CAMP:** 1. Bring water to boil.
⅓ C. powdered milk	2. Shake bag to ensure ingredients are well mixed.
4 – 5 C. water	3. Place 3 Tbsp of mix in a cup and fill with 8 oz boiling water.
	4. Stir until dissolved.
	5. Repeat for each serving.

Bannock is fried or skillet bread.

Kumbu French Toast

Who said eating "pain perdu" is the lost bread? We found it and its yummy.

4 eggs

⅔ C. milk

2 tsp cinnamon

8 thick slices 2 day old bread

2 Tbsp butter or oil

CONDIMENTS:
- Butter
- Maple syrup
- Fresh berries

AT CAMP:

1. In shallow bowl, beat eggs, milk and cinnamon.

2. Dip each slice of bread into mixture, allowing bread to soak up the liquid.

3. In large skillet over medium heat, melt butter or vegetable oil.

4. Add bread pieces; fry until brown on both sides.

5. Serve hot with butter, maple syrup and fresh berries.

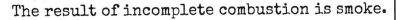

The result of incomplete combustion is smoke.

OWYHEE COUNTRY

THE NAME APPLIED TO THESE MOUNTAINS AND THE WHOLE SURROUNDING REGION IS AN OUTDATED SPELLING OF THE WORD "HAWAII".

Fur-trading ships brought Hawaiian natives--then called Owyhees--to the Northwest. In 1818, Donald Mackenzie brought the first big brigade of fur hunters to the Snake river valley. He sent several Owyhees to trap in this region --and they never came back. Ever since then, this has been called the Owyhee country, and Owyhee county carries the name on. (Pronounce Owyhee and Hawaii aloud--they sound the same.)

Owyhee Spam & Eggs

Hawaiians eat it and so do the people in Owyhee county.

6 oz (2 single serving) packets Spam	**AT HOME:**
	1. Put eggs into a camping/hiking egg carrier.
2 sun-dried tomato halves chopped finely	**2.** Put sun-dried tomatoes and cheese into bag.
	3. Place oil into spill-proof container.
4 eggs *2 Tbsp parmesan or romano cheese*	**AT CAMP:**
	1. Add oil to pan.
2 Tbsp Oil	**2.** Add Spam.
	3. Fry until brown.
	4. Add eggs and tomatoes.
	5. Scramble and stir until cooked.
	6. Top with cheese.
	NOTE: You can substitute powdered eggs.

Eating chocolate tends to make you thirsty.

Shrimp Sesame Noodles

Very fast and satisfying.

1 pkg (3 oz) shrimp flavor ramen

2 Tbsp dried diced carrots

2 Tbsp dried diced onions

¼ tsp red pepper flakes

1 pouch shrimp 8 oz

2 tsp sesame oil

1½ C. water

NOTE:
Can of tiny shrimp or freeze-dried shrimp may be substituted

AT HOME:
1. Pack ramen with ¼ of seasoning packet, and dry ingredients in a quart freezer bag.

2. Pack oil in small bottle.

3. Place it and the shrimp into the bag.

AT CAMP:
1. Add near boiling water to the bag.

2. Push out air, seal well and mix gently by shaking and rolling bag until ramen starts to soften.

3. Put bag into cozy 10 minutes, tucking shrimp packet underneath and ¼ C. near boiling water to sauce bag.

4. Drain water, add shrimp and toss with sesame oil.

Keep the water in your canteen cooler by wrapping the canteen in foil.

Smoked Salmon Chowder

Quick pick me up from the West Coast.

¼ C. dried, canned smoked salmon

¼ C. dried peas and carrot mix

⅛ C. powdered coconut milk

Dried dill (to taste)

Dash of curry (optional)

Salt and pepper to taste

AT HOME:
1. Combine all ingredients and place into Ziploc bag.

AT CAMP:
1. Place ingredients in a pot and add enough water to just cover.

2. Let sit 5 – 10 minutes to rehydrate.

3. Bring to boil and place into cozy for 5-10 minutes.

4. Add water to desired consistency.

5. Add additional seasonings to taste.

NOTE: Good if served with mashed sweet potatoes!

Channel lock pliers make good pot holders. Its worth the weight to carry them.

NEW ORLEANS

First sighted as Indian portage to Lake Pontchartrain and Gulf in 1699 by Bienville and Iberville. Founded by Bienville in 1718; named by him in honor of the Duke of Orleans, Regent of France. Called the Crescent City because of location in bend of the Mississippi.

ERECTED B

Spicy Cheesy Beans and Rice

New Orleans, we have arrived.

½ C. instant rice

¼ C. cooked and dehydrated kidney beans

¼ C. freeze-dried okra

2 Tbsp cheddar cheese powder

1 Tbsp powdered milk

1 packet Tabasco sauce

1 T (or 1 packet) olive oil

1 C. water

AT HOME:
1. Pack dry ingredients in sealable bag; tuck in Tabasco and olive oil.

AT CAMP:
1. Bring water and oil to boil; add dry ingredients.

2. Remove from heat; cover tightly and let sit for 10 min; add Tabasco sauce.

To protect your feet from blisters, smear soap on the inside of your inner sock at the heel and underneath the toes.

Don't Mess With Texas

UP TO $2000 FINE
FOR LITTERING

Tejano Medley

Texican's would be proud.

1 can black beans, drained and rinsed
1 can sweet corn, drained
1 medium chopped onion
2 small avocados, diced
2 C. salsa or diced fresh tomatoes
1 clove finely minced garlic
1 bunch cilantro, chopped
3 Tbsp lime juice
salt and pepper to taste

1. Combine all and let sit for 5 minutes.

Enjoy with pita bread, tortillas or chips.

Wind from Northeast is a likely an indication of a storm.

鷹取山

浦駅

京急田浦駅

Teriyaki Chicken

Yummy, who has the rice?

Ingredients	Instructions
2 C. dry instant rice	**AT HOME:**
	1. Mix dry ingredients; store in sealable bag.
½ tsp garlic powder	
	2. Store honey and soy packets and canned chicken in separate, dry container.
½ tsp ginger powder	
	AT CAMP:
1 packet honey (1 Tbsp)	1. Boil water; add dry mixture.
	2. After rice is cooked, stir in chicken, honey and soy.
2 packet soy (2 Tbsp)	
1½ C. water	
1 (5 oz) can chicken	

To keep mosquitoes away rub the inside of an orange peel on face, arms and legs.

Thai Chicken Rice

On the trail or off river, one pot no time.
This is wonderful.

1 pkg "Taste of Thai" coconut ginger soup base

1 pkg (7 Oz) chicken

1 chicken bouillon cube, crushed

3 Tbsp coconut crème powder

2 C. jasmine rice (pre-cooked and dehydrated)

Dried or fresh cilantro (optional)

½ C. + 2 C. water

AT HOME:
1. Package bouillon and coconut crème together in sealable bag.
2. Pack rice, chicken and soup mix separately.
3. If using cilantro, pack into separate bag.

AT CAMP:
1. Add ½ C. water to cover rice and rehydrate 5-10 minutes.
2. Bring 2 C. water to boil; turn off heat and mix in first packet ingredients.
3. Add soup mix and return to heat; bring to boil; cook 2 minutes.
4. In a bowl, add rice, chicken and the amount of soup you wish to mix in.
5. Add cilantro for garnish and a touch of flavor.

To remove musty smell from canteen, put three teaspoons of baking soda into the canteen with a bit of water.

The Extraordinary Bagel Sandwich

Might as eat well, no time to stop and cook something.

Lunch meat – ham, turkey, beef or other

Preferred type of sliced cheese

Sliced tomatoes – romas are best

Sliced sweet onions

Lettuce

Pickles

"Santa Barbara Tangy Apple" salsa

Very large baggy, or use foil

At Home:

1. To ensure freshness and to prevent sogginess, assembly is key. Careful construction 'waterproofs' the bagel against moisture of condiments and ingredients.

2. Onto ½ of each bagel, place your choice of lunch meat and top with slice of preferred cheese and "Santa Barbara Tangy Apple Salsa".

3. Onto second ½ of the bagel, place lettuce, tomatoes, onions and pickles (some prefer pickles on the side so place in separate baggie).

4. Put bagel halves together and place into zip lock bags or foil for a yummy treat on trail.

Purple or blackish seeds on grasses may be indicative of a toxic fungus.

Toasted Almond Rice & Chicken

Throw in some hot mustard and you are in a Chinese Restaurant.

1 small can (5 oz) boneless chicken packed in water

1⅓ C. instant rice (recommend brown)

⅓ C. sliced almonds

1 C. freeze-dried corn or peas or combination of both

2 Tbsp onion flakes

1 4 gram cube chicken bouillon or favorite soup mix

Salt & pepper to taste

AT HOME:

1. Spread nuts on baking sheet.

2. Bake at 300° for 8-10 minutes.

3. Cool and place into ziplock bag.

4. Package freeze-dried veggies, rice, onion flakes and bouillon into another ziplock bag.

AT CAMP:

1. Put chicken, veggie, rice, spice packet into pot with enough water to cover.

2. Bring to boil and simmer 6-7 minutes, adding additional water if needed.

3. Remove from heat; add nuts, mix and enjoy.

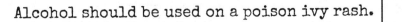

Alcohol should be used on a poison ivy rash.

Tomato Tortellini

Tomato and cheesy goodness.

1 pkg. (16 oz) tortellini pasta	**AT CAMP:** **1.** Bring water to a boil; add tortellini.
1 qt. water	**2.** Boil 10 minutes or until "al dente".
½ C. sun dried tomatoes, chopped	**3.** Add tomatoes and cook one minute.
	4. Drain water and add spice packet.
1 pkg Italian style spaghetti seasoning	**5.** Season with garlic powder or garlic salt.
Garlic salt or powder (to taste)	**6.** Mix well and enjoy!

Canning rings can be used to cook your eggs in for egg sandwiches.

Trailhead Tortilla Ramen

Use what you have or lose it.

CLASS 2

1 pkg (3oz) ramen (save flavor packet for later use)
1 tsp low sodium chicken bouillon
1 tsp Mexican or fajita seasoning blend
¼ tsp True lime powder (1 packet)
1 tsp diced dried carrots
1 tsp dried onion
1 tsp diced dried bell pepper
1 tsp diced sun-dried tomatoes
¼ C. corn chips
2 C. water

OPTIONAL:
Once cooked, top with corn chips

AT HOME:
1. Place ramen and dry seasonings into sealable ziploc bag.

2. Put chips into separate bag.

3. Top with corn chips.

AT CAMP:
Open pot method:
1. Bring water to boil; add all ingredients.

2. Simmer 10 minutes.

Smoking and drinking are the two "vices" which makes it more difficult to adjust to high altitudes.

APPALACHIAN TRAIL
Elevation Here 3400
Enjoy a short hike along a
portion of this famous trail,
a 2000 mile footpath from
Maine to Georgia.

Apple-lachion Brown Betty

The easiest dessert ever on the trail.

⅛ C. apple slices, dried

¼ C. raisins

½ C. bread crumbs

2 tsp sugar

¼ tsp cinnamon

½ C. water

*[Optional:
Crunchy Granola]*

*Variation:
Substitute chili
dried mango
slices for the ap-
ples, reduce
bread crumbs to ¼
cup, and keep
everything else
the same*

At Home:
1. Pack dried apples and raisins together in a small ziploc bag.

2. Pack bread crumbs in separate plastic bag.

3. Combine sugar and cinnamon in 2x3 plastic bag.

4. Place all bags into one larger re-sealable bag

On the Trail:
1. Place apples, raisins, sugar, and cinnamon in a small pot and add water to cover.

2. Light stove and maintain low flame until apple slices are soft and warm.

3. Stir in bread crumbs.

NOTE: The bread crumbs will absorb the sweet juices.
Top with crunchy granola.

Don't forget the heavy duty aluminum foil. There are many uses for it at camp.

Backpacking Biscuits

Perfect for Soup or Chowder.

2 C. biscuit mix

¼ C. powdered milk

½ C. water

½ tsp dried parsley

1 Tbsp freeze dried corn

3 single serving packets romano or parmesan cheese

AT HOME:
1. Combine all ingredients except water into quart size ziploc bag.

AT CAMP:
1. Gently stir water into bag; knead until dough forms.

2. Roll dough onto foil and make into biscuit shapes.

3. Cook on pan, turning as they brown.

CLASS 3

For ease of clean up and to protect from smoke and fire damage, put liquid soap on outside of your pots and pans before putting over the fire.

Biddle's Backpacking Bars

Perfect and easy to take on the trail.

CLASS 1

CLASS 2

CLASS 3

CLASS 4

CLASS 5

¾ C. all purpose flour
½ C. Quick Oats (uncooked)
½ C. butter – softened
¼ C. toasted wheat germ
1 Tbsp orange peel – zested
½ C. brown sugar—tightly packed
2 eggs
4½ oz blanched almonds – whole
½ C. shredded coconut

1. Preheat oven to 350.

2. In large bowl with mixer at low speed beat first 5 ingredients.

3. Add ¼ C. of the brown sugar and beat 2 minutes at medium speed (mixture will look dry).

4. With lightly floured hands, shape mixture into a ball, then pat into 8"by 8" baking pan.

5. In small bowl with hand beater, beat eggs with remaining ¼ C. brown sugar; stir in almonds and coconut.

6. Pour evenly over mixture in pan.

7. Bake 35 minutes or until toothpick comes out clean.

8. Cool in pan on rack.

9. Cut into 12 pieces and put into small sealable plastic bags for the trail.

When your body shivers it creates heat.

Boy Scout Pizza Rice

Cook it, put it down and step back or you'll be eaten!

1 5 oz pkg pepperoni slices
2 C. Minute Rice
2 C. Water
1 6 oz can diced tomatoes
2 Tbsp parmesan cheese
¼ C. mozzarella cheese
1 Tbsp minced garlic
2 Tbsp olive oil

OPTIONAL:
canned mushroom
black olives
(sliced or whole)

AT HOME:

1. Put the portioned rice, grated cheeses, optional vegetables and minced garlic into ziploc bag.

2. Place both oil and tomatoes into separate spill-proof containers.

AT CAMP:

1. Add oil, garlic and pepperoni to pan.

2. Heat on medium high heat 1 minute; remove and set aside.

3. Pour 2 C. water into pot; bring to boil.

4. Add rice and cook 1 minute.

5. Remove from heat; add garlic and pepperoni; stir.

6. Add optional items; stir and add cheese.

To cook hamburgers more evenly throughout, put a hole in the middle of your hamburger about the size of your finger, during grilling the hole will disappear but the center will be cooked the same as the edges.

Bryan's Healthy Turtles

The healthiest guy I know, these taste better than healthy.

4 C. "Nature's Path" "Pumpkin Flax Plus Granola" cereal
2 C. rolled oats
2 C. raisins
1 C. ground raw almonds
1 C. dark chocolate chips (60% cocoa or better)
4 Tbsp ground flax seeds
1 C. fat free sweetened condensed milk

1. Mix well and spread on 13x 17.5 inch cookie sheet about 3/8" thick.

2. Bake 45 minutes at 250 degrees.

3. Cut into squares after removing from oven and let cool.

4. Remove bars from cookie sheet with spatula.

Ice should be boiled before using it as a source of drinking water.

Campout Quickie Pasta

If this pots rockin, don't bother knockin.

1 bag 12 oz egg noodles

1 5 oz can roast beef shredded

1 10.5 oz can beef gravy

Water

Salt and pepper to taste

AT CAMP:
1. Cook noodles in water (according to package instructions).

2. Drain; add beef and gravy.

3. Add salt and pepper.

If you wear a hat, your hands and feet will stay warmer.

Cashew Rice Curry

Take out in the backcountry.

Ingredients	AT CAMP:
¼ C. powdered milk	**1.** Mix powdered milk and enough water to form a paste.
½ tsp salt	**2.** Add remaining water; mix well and bring to a boil.
1 tsp curry powder	**3.** Stir in rice and curry.
3½ C. water	**4.** Cover and simmer until water is absorbed and rice is soft (approx. 20 minutes).
2 C. instant rice	**5.** Stir in nuts and cheese.
¼ C. cashew pieces	**6.** Serve when cheese is melted pan.
2 oz grated cheddar cheese	

Single Use Salve Packs: Make these with drinking straws and your choice of ointments and salves.

Chicken Poppers

I wonder what Dave Thomas would think?

Ingredients	Instructions
1 lb chicken tenders	**AT CAMP:**
	1. Cut jalapeños in half, removing all seeds and membrane.
10 large jalapeños	**2.** Place 1 chicken tender in pepper.
1 pkg bacon	**3.** Wrap with bacon.
foil	**4.** Place all on foil and wrap.
	5. Cook on grill approx. 20 minutes.

Clever Night Lamp: Make this with a plastic milk jug filled with water and wrapped with a headlamp.

Corny Cakes

Candy corn is my favorite vegetable.

1 pkg Jiffy corn muffin mix

1 egg

1 Tbsp melted shortening

¾ C. milk

Stick of butter or margarine

OPTION: Serve with bacon or sausage

AT CAMP:

1. Add shortening to hot griddle.

2. Mix ingredients together; and spoon onto griddle.

3. Turn pancakes when bubbles appear.

4. Top with butter or margarine and favorite breakfast meat, syrup or other.

Flour doesn't have greater thickening power than cornstarch.

Couscous and Chicken

Sounds fancy and it is!

1 C. couscous
1 small package (⅜ C.) dried mushrooms, any type you like
⅜ C. chopped dried tomatoes (optional)
⅜ C. raisins (optional)
¼ pine nuts, toasted or sliced almonds
2 tsps chicken bouillon granules
2 Tbsps minced dried onions
1 Tbsp dried parsley
1 tsp dried basil
¼ tsp ground turmeric
⅛ tsp black pepper
1 5 oz can chicken meat

AT HOME:
1. Make a packet of the spices, mushrooms, tomatoes and raisins.

2. Put couscous and pine nuts in separate baggies.

AT CAMP:
1. Bring 2 to 2½ cups water to a boil.

2. Add mushroom/spice packet and let sit off the heat a few minutes to rehydrate mushrooms and tomatoes. Adjust salt as needed.

3. Bring back to a boil and add canned chicken and couscous, stir briefly to combine.

4. Remove from heat and cover until all water is absorbed. If too dry add a little more hot water and let sit a couple of minutes.

5. Sprinkle with toasted pine nuts before serving.

Protect toilet paper from rain and dirt by storing in a plastic tub (like a Folgers Coffee container).

Hyndman Cheesy Baco-Spuds

Triumphant Pioneers

2¼ C. instant potatoes
½ C. powdered milk
1 packet Butter Buds
1½ Tbsp dried parsley flakes
1¼ Tbsp dried Onions
¾ C. cooked and crumbled bacon
1 pkg powdered cheese (or substitute fresh cheese)
Salt and pepper to taste
4½ C. water (slightly less if using fresh cheese)

AT HOME:

1. Add all dry ingredients into quart size Ziploc freezer bag.

AT CAMP:

1. Bring water to boil; add to bag.

2. Stir well; let stand and add more water if needed.

Try spraying "Original" Listerine around the campsite to repel mosquitoes.

Island Shrimp Rice

Mahalo

Ingredients	Instructions
¼ C. shrimp, dried	**AT HOME:** 1. Combine dry ingredients and place into Ziploc bag.
⅛ C. dried pineapple	2. Press air out and seal
⅛ C. bell peppers, assorted colors, dried	**AT CAMP:** 1. Add contents of bag to pot with water; allow to rehydrate 5-10 minutes.
½ tsp dry coconut	2. Bring to a boil and continue cooking with lid on at medium to high heat for 1-2 minutes.
½ C instant white or brown rice	
1 C. water	3. Don't stir rice!
	4. Place pot into insulated cozy and wait 10 minutes for the meal to continue rehydrating.

Dingle stick is used to hold a pot over a campfire.

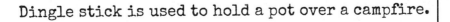

King Ludd's Phad Thai

Eat it all, you might not want leftovers for your critter friends.

1 box "Taste of Thai" rice noo-dles	**AT CAMP:** **1.** Boil noodles according to package instructions.
2 packs clams (in foil packs near tuna at grocery store)	**2.** Add clams and sauce one minute before end of cooking time.
1 pkg "Sunbird" Phad Thai sauce, dry	**3.** Garnish with nuts and cilantro.
¼ C. crushed peanuts and cashews	
1 small bunch cilantro, chopped	

Body heat should be applied directly to a frostbitten area.

La Toison

105 E4

LAMPEDUSA 2

Lampedusa Basil Parmesan Orzo

Does this remind someone I know of toga parties?

¼ tsp butter flakes

½ C. orzo pasta

1 tsp dried basil

½ tsp dried parsley

2 Tbsp freeze-dried corn

3 packets parmesan or romano cheese

1 – 1½ C. water

AT HOME:
1. Combine all but cheese in quart size Ziploc bag.

AT CAMP:
1. Bring water to boil.

2. Add bag ingredients.

3. Simmer 5 minutes or until pasta is cooked.

4. Add more water if needed for desired consistency.

5. Stir in cheese just before serving.

Acorns from the white oak and pin oak may be eaten raw if desired.

Lemon Tuna Spaghetti

Olive you!

8 oz spaghetti
pasta, broken
into thirds
1 Tbsp olive oil
(or one packet)
¼ C. Kalamata
olives, chopped
3 Tbsp lemon
juice (3 packets
or one lemon)
3 oz pouch
albacore tuna
¼ C. seasoned
bread crumbs
¼ C. shelf stable
parmesan cheese
1 tsp dried
parsley
¼ tsp ground
black pepper
4 C. water

AT HOME:
1. Pack spaghetti into sandwich bag.

2. Place breadcrumbs, cheese, parsley and pepper into snack bag.

3. Carry everything else in separate snack bags.

AT CAMP:
1. Bring water to boil.

2. Add pasta and cook for time on pkg; drain, reserving ½ of the water.

3. Add oil, olives, lemon juice, tuna and reserved water to the pot.

4. Toss to combine.

5. Sprinkle with breadcrumbs and toss to combine.

Contrary to what you might think, eggs keep quite well on a camping trip.

Lentil Soft Tacos

Who woulda thought you could make tacos with Lentils?

⅓ C. instant rice
¼ C. cooked and dehydrated lentils
1 Tbsp diced dried bell peppers
1 Tbsp diced sun-dried tomatoes
1 Tbsp diced dried onions
1 tsp **tomato powder**
⅛ tsp sugar
⅛ tsp salt
⅛ tsp garlic powder
1 packet True Lemon powder
2 soft tortillas (small)
1 oz queso fresco cheese
1 C. water

AT HOME:
1. Pack instant rice in qt size ziploc bag.

2. Pack remaining ingredients in another pint bag, cheese in its own separate bag.

3. Wrap bags in larger bag with tortillas.

AT CAMP:
1. Bring 1 C. water to boil; add ½ C. water to rice bag; stir and seal tightly.

2. Add ½ C. water to bag with lentils and spices.

3. Stir well and seal tightly.

4. Place both bags into cozy for 15 minutes.

5. Crumble or dice the cheese and top tortillas with the fillings and cheese and fold.

Are flies a nuisance? Try hanging clear plastic bags filled with water from tree branches.

Lisa's Last Minute Pizza

Pick it up on the way out of town.

1 twin pack 8"
Boboli pizza
shells
1 (5 oz) Boboli
pizza
sauce pouch
½ pkg (1½ oz)
pepperoni slices
2 pieces (2 oz)
string cheese
8 olives of choice
(from store olive
bar)
2 Tbsp or 2
packets olive oil
2 paper towels

NOTE:
For truly last
minute prepara-
tion, pick up all
items at the
grocery store on
the way to your
adventure!

AT HOME:
1. Pack olive oil in spill proof container.

AT CAMP:
1. Lay paper towels down as clean work surface.

2. Divide pizza sauce between the two shells.

3. Top each with pepperoni and chopped olives and cheese.

4. Using a wide fry pan lid or 2 liter pot, heat ½ oil over low flame and place each shell into oil.

5. Add ½ oil and place each shell into oil.

6. Cover tightly and heat gently.

7. Allow pizzas to rest before cutting.

CLASS 3

Use an old leather belt and S-hooks to hang gear high around a tree trunk.

Mushroom Soup Meatballs

Mama Mia

Ingredients	Instructions
Ground meat	**AT HOME:** **1.** Shape onions, meat and spices into meatballs.
Dried onions	
Basil, thyme and salt and pepper to taste	**2.** Place into Ziploc bag.
1 can cream of mushroom soup	**AT CAMP:** **1.** Add oil to skillet.
3 Tbsp oil	**2.** Place meatballs into skillet and cook until brown on all sides.
2 lbs of ground beef	**3.** Add soup diluted with ½ can water to skillet.
½ C. dried onions	**4.** Cook until soup is liquid and smooth.
	Serve over toast, egg noodles or rice.

CLASS 1
CLASS 2
CLASS 3
CLASS 4
CLASS 5

Toothpaste Dots: Once they're dry you can pop one in your mouth, chew a bit, sip some water then start brushing.

Sesame Orange Chicken

Better make double.

Ingredients	Instructions
1 C. instant rice	**AT HOME:**
	1. Pack rice into quart freezer bag.
2 tsp toasted sesame seeds	**2.** In second bag, pack the other ingredients.
1 tsp dry milk	
1 tsp low sodium chicken bouillon	**3.** Tuck the chicken in with the bags.
	AT CAMP:
½ tsp butter powder	**1.** Add chicken and ¼ C. near boiling water to sauce bag.
½ tsp cornstarch	**2.** Seal tightly and put into a cozy 15 minutes.
¼ tsp orange drink mix (such as Crystal Light or Tang)	**3.** Add 1 C. near boiling water to rice bag.
⅛ tsp red pepper powder	**4.** Seal tightly and put into cozy with sauce bag.
	5. Fluff rice and serve sauce over rice.
1 can (5 oz) chicken	
1¼ C. water	

All powdered drinks are welcome at camp sites. Avoid liquid forms, except for water. This will make your carrying load lighter and more convenient. The most common drink options are hot chocolate, instant tea and coffee.

Spicy Tuna Linguine

The perfect meal to have after wandering around lost all day. Not that I'm speaking from experience...

8 oz linguine pasta
½ tsp granulated garlic
¼ tsp red pepper flakes
¼ tsp ground black pepper
¼ tsp dried oregano
2 Tbsp (or 2 packets) olive oil
3 oz albacore tuna pouch
2 Tbsp dry bread crumbs (plain or Italian flavored)
2 Tbsp shelf-stable parmesan cheese
4 C. water

NOTES:
Substitute oil packed tuna or 5 oz "pop-top" canned tuna

AT HOME:

1. Break pasta in half and pack into sealable bag.

2. Pack seasonings into sealable bag.

3. Combine bread crumbs and cheese; pack into sealable bag.

4. Tuck oil packets and tuna into one of the sealable bags.

AT CAMP:

1. Add oil to seasoning bag; seal and massage lightly.

2. Bring 4 C. water to boil; add pasta and cook per bag directions (approx. 9 minutes).

3. Drain water; reserve ½ C.

4. Toss pasta with tuna and seasonings and then with breadcrumb mix.

5. Add reserved water as needed to coat pasta.

You have been spotted by a search plane when the pilot wiggles the wings of the plane.

Splattski Salmon Pesto Pasta

Backpacking Gourmet at it best.

1 lb pasta
(linguini,
spaghetti, angel
hair or other)

1 foil pack of
salmon (you'll
find this in the
canned fish aisle
at your grocery
store)

1 pkg Knorr®
pesto sauce

AT CAMP:

1. Bring water to a boil.

2. Cook pasta to al dente (firm).

3. Follow direction of sauce packet to prepare sauce.

4. Combing pesto and salmon to the pasta. Mix and serve.

Proteins are necessary to maintain and
repair the body condition. You can burn up to 8,000 calories
per day when winter camping.

CLASS 1

CLASS 2

CLASS 3

CLASS 4

CLASS 5

Trail Pancakes

*Add blueberries or huckleberries and
invite the bears for breakfast.*

1 C. Bisquick
1 Tbsp powdered
milk
1 tbsp sugar
$\frac{2}{3}$ C. water
1 Tbsp squeeze
margarine
1 Tbsp cooking
oil

NOTE: instead of
squeeze mar-
garine, you may
substitute
vegetable oil

AT HOME:
1. Add Bisquick, milk and sugar into
quart size Ziploc bag.

2. Seal and shake well.

AT CAMP:
1. Add water and margarine to bag; seal
and roll the bag by hand to remove air
and lumps.

2. Add oil to pan; heat to medium high
temperature.

3. Cut hole in corner of the bag and
squeeze pancake size amount into hot
pan.

4. Cook until bubbles form; flip and
cook until golden brown.

Condensation on the wall of a tent is less likely
to occur on a breezy night.

Tuna Spaghetti

Only the best Charlie gets to be tuna.

Ingredients	Instructions
1 – 8 oz pkg angel hair pasta	**AT HOME:** 1. Mix basil oregano, cheese and garlic powder; place into Ziploc bag.
1 – 6 oz can or packet of tuna in oil	2. Store other items separately.
8 dried tomato halves, sliced	**AT CAMP:** 1. Soak tomatoes in 4 C water for 10 minutes to rehydrate.
1 tsp dried basil	2. Remove from water and bring water to boil.
1 tsp oregano	3. Break pasta in half and add to the water.
¼ C. parmesan cheese	4. Cook until done; drain.
½ tsp garlic powder	5. To noodles in pot, add tuna, tomatoes, cheese and spices.
	6. Stir well.

Dotted lines on National Forest maps symbolize trails.

133

Tuna Wraps

A meal you don't have to stop on the trail for.

1 (3 oz) packet tuna

1 mayonnaise condiment packet

1 relish condiment packet

2 flour tortillas

AT HOME OR CAMP:

1. Open tuna packet.

2. Mix in mayonnaise and relish.

3. Spread onto tortillas.

4. Roll and cut into rounds.

Always have a large poncho. It works not just for rain, but for carrying water and as an emergency dropcloth.

135

Beef Curry Noodle Bowl

Mongolian BBQ for the trail.

½ C. chopped jerky (regular or peppered)
½ C. dried vegetable mix
¼ C. raisins
1 Tbsp mild curry powder
4 tsp low sodium beef bouillon
1 tsp granulated garlic
5 oz pkg chukka soba noodles, crumbled
4 C. water

Dried vegetable mix can be found in bulk food sections or use freeze-dried such as Just Vegetables;

AT HOME:
1. Pack everything but the noodles a sandwich bag.

2. Pack noodles in separate bag.

AT CAMP:
1. Bring water to a boil; add noodles; return to a boil; simmer 3 minutes.

2. Remove from stove; cover; let sit 5 minutes.

3. Season to taste with salt and pepper.

NOTE: Chuka soba noodles (also called chow mein noodles) can be found in the Asian section of stores); angel hair pasta may be substituted or 2 pkgs ramen noodles (without seasoning packet).

Longitudes run east and west.

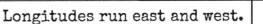

Buckaroo Casserole

I have enjoyed this after a long trail ride. Cowboy Up!

½ lb bacon

1 lb ground beef

1 small onion, chopped

2 - 15 oz each cans baked beans with pork

⅓ C. barbeque sauce

1 (7.5 oz) pkg refrigerated biscuit dough

AT HOME or AT CAMP:

1. Cook bacon in large skillet or Dutch oven over medium heat until evenly browned.

2. Drain and cut into bite sized pieces; set aside.

3. Add meat and onion to the skillet and cook until no longer pink and onion is tender; drain.

4. Stir bacon, beans, and sauce into the meat and bring to a boil.

5. Reduce heat to medium low; place biscuits in single layer over the top of the mixture.

6. Cover and simmer about 10 min. or until biscuits are brown.

7. Place two biscuits on each plate and spoon beans over.

Use lamp oil on your legs to prevent chiggers. Chiggers tunnel into your flesh to lay their eggs.

Buffalo Chicken Wraps

Buffalos can't fly!

⅓ C. couscous
1 tsp diced dried onion
1 tbsp diced freeze-dried celery
2 tsp bleu cheese powder
⅛ tsp low sodium chicken bouillon
1 packet hot sauce
1 pkg (7 oz) chicken
1 large flour tortilla
⅛ C. water

AT HOME:
1. Put dry ingredients, hot sauce, chicken and tortillas into quart freezer bag.

AT CAMP:
1. Remove chicken packet and hot sauce packet from freezer bag.

2. Add ¼ C. near boiling water to the freezer bag then add chicken.

3. Seal tightly and put into a cozy for 5-10 minutes or until liquid is absorbed.

4. Spread mixture on tortilla and drizzle with hot sauce.

"Fool's Gold" is another name for iron pyrite.

140

Camp Onion Rings

Better than an appetizer at Applebee's.

1 large Vidalia (or Bermuda) onion
1 pkg pancake mix
Water (according to pkg directions)
1 stick butter flavored Crisco stick
Salt and pepper to taste

NOTES:
Salt and pepper may be added to batter as it's sweet, particularly when using Vadalia onions, or use seasoned salt, Essence of Emeril, Lemon or Cayenne pepper if substituting red or white Bermuda onions to make spicier rings

AT CAMP:
1. Peel then slice onion into desired ring size.

2. Mix batter into water (to make thinner than what you'd make for pancakes).

3. Heat Crisco in skillet.

4. Coat rings with batter.

5. Fry to golden brown; drain on paper towels.

A "col" is a mountain pass.

Camp Tiramisu

Thank you Brother Matt, for this inspiration.

$2\frac{1}{3}$ C. water

2 tsp instant espresso powder

2 Tbsp Kahlua (Pick up a minibottle at the liquor store.)

3.4 oz packet instant white chocolate pudding

$\frac{2}{3}$ C. powdered milk

12 ladyfingers

1 dark chocolate bar

AT HOME:
1. Pack all ingredients separately in small bags or reusable containers.

ON THE TRAIL:
1. Heat $\frac{1}{3}$ cup of water to a boil and then mix in espresso and Kahlua.

2. Make pudding in separate bowl according to package directions using powdered milk and 2 cups of water.

3. Place six ladyfingers in the bottom of a pot or bowl, drizzle half of the espresso mixture over them and then spread half of the pudding on top.

4. Place six more ladyfingers on top and then repeat espresso mixture and pudding to create a second layer.

5. Use a pocketknife to shave thin strips of chocolate form candy bar, and sprinkle these over the tiramisu.
Serves 2-3.

CLASS 1

CLASS 2

CLASS 3

CLASS 4

CLASS 5

Fill your water bottle with boiling hot water, wrap it in a towel, and put it in your sleeping bag a few minutes before you climb in. This makes for cozy sleeping quarters.

Carne Asada with Sherrie's Cilantro Lime Rice

A little bit of 'Ol Mexico in the backcountry.

Minute Rice (use box guide for 4 servings)
One bunch fresh cilantro, rough chopped
Jalapeños (to taste)
4 packets Weber® Chipotle Marinade Mix
4 large flour tortillas
Juice of 3 limes
2 cloves garlic
1 lb thinly sliced skirt steak
2 Tbsp olive oil
One 12" x 12" piece of foil

EQUIPMENT:
• Camp stove
• One boiler pot

AT HOME:

1. Mix marinade according to package directions; marinate steak overnight in refrigerator or in 1 gallon freezer bag and freeze for the trip.

2. Dice jalapeños and garlic; chop cilantro; place into separate ziplock bags.

AT CAMP:

1. To hot pan with olive oil, add steak and cook to desired doneness; wrap in foil to retain heat.

2. Wipe out pot; add olive oil, garlic and jalapeños; bring to sizzle.

3. Add water (amount per box instructions), ½ of cilantro and the lime juice; bring to boil.

4. Add minute rice; turn off heat and cover
5-7 minutes.

5. Serve on tortillas or in bowls; garnish with remaining cilantro.

CLASS 1
CLASS 2
CLASS 3
CLASS 4
CLASS 5

If you have ended the day with a pair of wet socks, sleep with them around your midsection. I know it sounds terrible, but your body heat during the night, coupled with the warmth of your sleeping bag, will dry them by morning.

Curried Salmon Pilaf

This is for you Sarah Simon.

1½ C. instant rice
¼ packet vegetable soup mix
2 tsp mild curry powder
2-3 oz pouch wild salmon
1 Tbsp extra virgin olive oil (1 packet)
½ C. fresh huckleberries
1½ C. water

NOTE:
You may substitute blueberries for huckleberries.

For One Pot Method:
In cooler weather, use a pot cozy to retain heat.

AT HOME:
1. Pack rice soup mix, curry, salmon and oil packets into quart freezer bag.

AT CAMP: Pick berries
1. Add water, oil and salmon to pot; boil.

2. Add rice; stir and fold in berries.

3. Cover tightly and set aside for 10 minutes.

Chewing gum will not stop dehydration.

Ginger Lemon Chicken

Winner Winner paired with Chicken Dinner White Wine

1 tsp diced dried onions

1 tsp low sodium chicken bouillon

1 tsp brown sugar

¼ tsp ground ginger

¼ tsp lemonade mix

½ tsp cornstarch

1 (5 oz) can chicken

1 packet soy sauce

¼ C. water

AT HOME:
1. Pack dry ingredients in quart freezer bag.

2. Put chicken and soy in separate bag.

AT CAMP:
1. Bring water to near boil.

2. Add to bag with dry ingredients.

3. Add chicken and soy.

4. Seal tightly and put in cozy for 15 minutes.

5. Serve over instant rice, ramen or mashed potatoes.

Use a pine cone or a handful of sand to scrub your dishes clean. That way you are not always searching for the dirty, smelly pot scrubby.

Grand Canyon Coleslaw

After a hot hike in the Grand Canyon, this cool cole slaw hits the spot.

3 heads of cabbage

12 scallions

2 bunch fresh cilantro, torn

1¼ C. sour cream

1¼ C. mayonnaise

5 Tbsp sugar

6 limes

AT HOME:
1. Shave the cabbage with a sharp knife or mandoline so you have thin strips. Cut the scallions long so you have pieces similar in shape to the cabbage.

2. Toss the cabbage, scallions and cilantro in a large salad bowl and put into a freezer bag or plastic container for travel in your cooler.

3. Make the dressing by combining the sour cream, mayonnaise, sugar and the zest of the limes in a medium bowl. Season with salt and pepper and finish with a squeeze of lime juice. Put in a container for travel in your cooler.

AT CAMP:
1. Pour the dressing over the cabbage mixture and toss to combine inside the freezer bag. Serve and enjoy.

Dirty socks increase the chance of blisters.

Grilled Onion Blossom

Outback in the backcountry.

1 large sweet onion

1¼ Tbsp butter

Garlic salt (to taste)

Ground black pepper (to taste)

Foil

AT CAMP:

1. Preheat outdoor grill to high heat.

2. Peel and slice onion into 8 wedges, leaving the base of the onion intact.

3. Pull apart wedges slightly and place butter, garlic salt and pepper inside onion.

4. Wrap onion tightly in foil.

5. Place on grill and cook 45 minutes or until onion is translucent and lightly browned.

Build your campfire away from tree and underbrush root systems. You might never guess, but these can also catch on fire.

Grilled Pepper Provolone Flatbread Pizza

Pizza Pizza Pizza Pie

1 Tbsp olive oil
salt and pepper
4 large naan
(flatbread)
2 halved red or
yellow bell
peppers
6 oz shredded
provolone
1 Tbsp olive oil
$\frac{1}{3}$ C. grated
parmesan (1$\frac{1}{2}$ oz)
$\frac{1}{2}$ tsp red pepper
flakes (optional)
2 Tbsp fresh
oregano or 1$\frac{1}{2}$
Tbsp dried

AT CAMP:

1. Preheat grill to medium- heat; clean and lightly oil grill.

2. Brush peppers with oil and season with salt and pepper.

3. Grill, covered until lightly charred and tender, approx. 4-5 min.

4. Transfer to cutting board; cut into thin slices.

5. Grill flatbread until undersides begin to char (1-2 minutes); flip and top with peppers, cheeses and red pepper flakes.

6. Season with salt and pepper, cover and cook until cheese melts, approx. 3-4 min.

7. Top with oregano and serve.

Rain is likely to occur if the trees are showing the undersides of their leaves.

Mel's Bow Tie Pasta

Tuxedo not required.

1 - 12 oz pkg bowtie pasta
2 Tbsp olive oil
3 cloves garlic
1 - 28 oz diced tomatoes (or 3.5 oz chopped sundried tomatoes)
1 lb Italian sausage
1½ C. cream (or powdered cream)
¼ tsp red pepper flakes
½ tsp salt
½ C. diced onion
3 Tbsp fresh parsley (optional)

AT HOME:
1. Mince garlic; dice onions; crumble sausage; chop parsley.
2. Place each into separate sealable bags; refrigerate.

AT CAMP:
1. Bring a large pot of lightly salted water to a boil.
2. Add pasta and cook until al dente (approx. 8-10 min.).
3. Heat oil in large, deep skillet over medium heat.
4. Cook sausage and pepper flakes until browned.
5. Stir in onion and garlic and cook until tender.
6. Stir in tomatoes, cream and salt.
7. Simmer until mixture thickens (approx. 8-10 min.).
8. Add cooked pasta into sauce; heat through. Garnish with parsley.

Eating snow causes loss of body heat.

Pancake Toast

It's conflicted.

Pancake mix (one cup per four people)

White bread (two slices per person)

Non-stick cooking spray or oil

Toppings:
Syrup, cinnamon, powdered sugar, fresh berries, butter or jam

AT CAMP:

1. Mix pancake mix with water according to package instructions.

2. Mix completely until slightly watery.

3. Spray pan or griddle with non-stick cooking spray or add oil.

4. Dip white bread into mix to cover both sides but not too long or bread will fall apart.

5. Place on griddle or fry pan until each side is done to desired toasty color.

6. Serve with choice of toppings.

Prechill your cooler by filling it with ice 30 minutes before adding food.

Pizza Biscuits

Can you really tell that it's not delivery or Digiorno?

1 C. baking mix
1 Tbsp Italian herb blend
$\frac{1}{2}$ tsp diced dried garlic
$\frac{1}{2}$ tsp ground black pepper
2 T olive oil (2 packets)
2 oz string cheese
1 packet shelf stable pepperonis slices
$\frac{1}{2}$ C. water

NOTE:
For cheese, any type may be substituted. Two ounces is 2 sticks of pre-wrapped.

AT HOME:
1. Mix dry ingredients; store in sealable bag.

2. Pack oil, cheese and meat in sealable bag.

AT CAMP:
1. Cube cheese and separate pepperoni slices.

2. Add cool water to dry ingredients bag and knead until dough forms.

3. Add cheese and meat and knead until combined.

PREPARATION TIPS:
A 2-liter pot can handle whole batch; if smaller, split and cook in half.
When doing half batches, split oil between two batches.

Soapy water can be used to test a camp stove for a fuel leak.

Ramen Pot Pie

I wonder if they had this is mind when they invented ramen noodles.

1 pkg chicken (or you're flavor preference) ramen noodles

1 can 3-5 oz chicken

1 pkg flavored instant mashed potatoes

2 C. water

AT HOME:
1. Pack ramen with ¼ – ½ of flavor packet in quart freezer items;

2. Put other ingredients in separate bag.

AT CAMP:
1. Add chicken and near boiling water to the ramen bag;

2. Seal tightly and put in cozy 10 minutes;

3. Slowly add dry potatoes, stirring until thick.

Darkening of the urine may be a sign of dehydration.

Sassy's
Sweet and Sour Chicken

Yes, she really is!

1 C. water	**AT HOME:**
½ C. vinegar	**1.** Directions to cook Sauce: Combine all ingredients minus the ketchup and bring to a boil, then add the ⅓ cup of
1 C. sugar	Ketchup.
1 Tsp salt	**2.** Cube chicken and put in freezer bag.
1 Tsp crushed red pepper seeds	**At Camp:**
	1. 1. Add oil and garlic to fry pan or pot, bring to medium heat add chicken
2 Tbsp corn starch	cubes and cook until done (About 5 minutes)
⅓ C. ketchup	**2.** Then add Bell Pepper and chopped into the chicken.
1 lb. of Chicken Breast meat	**3.** Add Sweet and Sour Sauce over the top and cook on low for 5 minutes.
1 bell pepper	
½ can pineapple chunks	**4.** Serve over steamed Rice (Minute Rice) and enjoy.

Open cell foam sleep pads absorb moisture.

Sausage Ragu Penne Pasta

A staple at home and at camp.

1 lb of Italian Sausage
3 Tbsp olive oil
¼ C. chopped celery
¼ C. diced onion
3 Tbsp diced garlic
2 - 30 oz cans diced tomatoes (drained)
3 Tbsp sugar
2 Tbsp dried oregano
1 C. chopped fresh basil
¼ C. chopped green bell pepper
¼ C. chopped yellow bell pepper
¼ C. chopped red bell pepper
1 lb. penne pasta
1 can medium size black olives chopped and (drained)
1 Tbsp red pepper flakes
¼ C. parmesan cheese for garnish
4 oz package of pepperoni

AT HOME:

1. Heat; add olive oil in fry pan; add celery, onions and garlic. Cook until tender.

2. In 4 qt pot, fry sausage until brown; drain fat; add vegetables add tomatoes to meat.

3. Bring to boil; turn to low heat; add basil, pepper flakes and oregano; simmer 3-4 minutes.

4. Add chopped peppers and olives; remove from heat.

5. Place all in freezer bag and freeze (for backpacking) or refrigerate (for car camping).

6. Boil pasta to al dente; drain; cool and place in freezer bag; refrigerate.

AT CAMP:

1. Heat sauce until warm; add pasta.

2. Top with parmesan.

Wheat bread doesn't smush up the way white bread does.

Slader
Double Cheese Taters

He's likes hims taters.

⅔ C. instant mashed potatoes
2 Tbsp sun-dried tomatoes, sliced thin
1 Tbsp powdered milk
1 Tbsp butter powder
1 Tbsp shelf stable parmesan cheese
¼ tsp granulated garlic
¼ tsp Italian seasoning
5 oz can chicken breast
1 packet string cheese
1 C. water

AT HOME:

1. Pack dry ingredients into quart freezer bag.

2. Tuck chicken and cheese stick into the bag.

AT CAMP:

1. Bring water to boil.

2. Add all ingredients (except cheese).

3. Remove from heat; stir in potato mixture.

4. Let sit covered 5 min.

5. Remove from heat and cover tightly for 15 min.

Your campfire should be fed from the lee side.

Spaghetti Olio (Aglio E Olio)

Thank you my "deer" friend Jeff!

Ingredients	AT CAMP:
1 lb dried spaghetti pasta	**1.** Bring ½ gallon water to boil; add pasta.
⅓ C. olive oil	**2.** Cook until firm (al dente).
1 Tbsp minced garlic	**3.** Drain pasta.
1 Tbsp dried parsley	**4.** Add oil to fry pan and add garlic; cook to light brown.
2 tsp red pepper flakes	**5.** Add pepper flakes to oil.
	6. Remove from heat, add parsley and pour over pasta.
	7. Mix well.

Natural odors become stronger during a low pressure front or area.

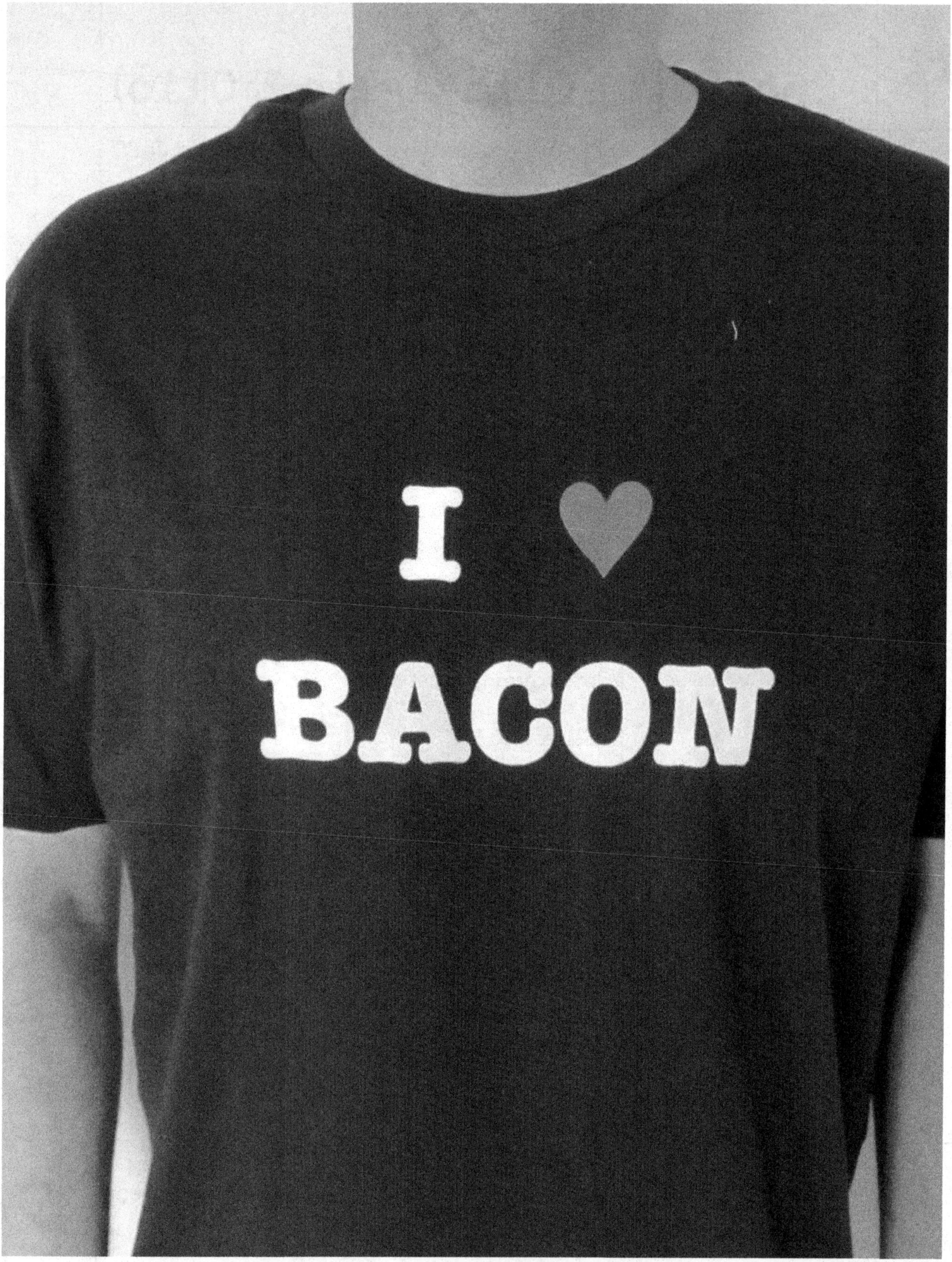
I ♥
BACON

Split Pea & Bacon Soup

Do I really need to add that everything is better with bacon? Even split pea soup!

⅓ C. cooked and dried split peas
2 Tbsp powdered milk
2 Tbsp shelf-stable bacon or bacon bits
1 Tbsp diced dried carrots
1 Tbsp dried or freeze dried hashbrowns (or mashed potatoes)
2 tsp low sodium chicken bouillon
1 tsp dehydrated onion
1 tsp dried parsley
½ tsp dried carrot powder
¼ tsp dried garlic
¼ tsp ground black pepper
¼ tsp dried chives
2 C. water

AT HOME:
1. Pack all ingredients into gallon ziploc bag.

AT CAMP:
1. Add boiling water to bag of dry mix; stir and let sit 15 – 30 minutes.

Insulated mug method:
1. Add boiling water to dry mix; seal container; let sit 15 – 30 minutes.

One pot method:
1. Add dry mix to boiling.
2. Remove from heat.
3. Let sit 15–30 minutes; in cold temperatures place into a cozy.

The Appalachian Trail is the longest continuously marked footpath in the world.

Tanner's Spam Fried Rice

Do not put ketchup on this.

1¼ C instant rice
¼ C. freeze-dried mixed vegetables
1 Tbsp dried chives
2 tsp low sodium bouillon (your flavor preference)
¼ tsp granulated garlic
¼ tsp dried powdered ginger
¼ tsp red pepper flakes
¼ tsp sugar
2 packets soy sauce
3 oz Spam single pack
1 Tbsp vegetable oil (on packet)
2 fresh eggs
2 C. water

AT HOME:
1. Pack rice, vegetables and seasonings in quart freezer bag.

2. Tuck soy sauce, oil and Spam into same bag.

AT CAMP:
1. Bring water to boil.

2. Add to rice bag; stir well; seal tightly and put into cozy for 15 minutes.

3. Heat oil over medium flame in non-stick trail wok or 2 liter pot pan and add Spam.

4. Cube up and stir fry until golden brown.

5. Add cooked rice and stir constantly.

6. Splash on soy sauce, toss and mix.

7. Make hole in center; crack eggs into hole. Scramble and toss with rice.

Lost? Moss usually grows on the North side of a tree.

Tuna Melt Wraps

Remember you can tune a piano but you can't tuna fish.

4 sheets (12x18-inches each) foil
1 can (12 oz.) tuna in water, drained
2 C. cooked rice
1 C. frozen baby green peas
½ C. light mayonnaise
1¼ C. shredded cheddar cheese, divided
1 Tbsp lemon pepper
4 (10-inch) flour tortillas

AT CAMP:

1. Preheat grill to medium-high indirect heat (for indirect heat, the heat source – coals or gas burner – is on one side of the grill. Place the foil packets on the opposite side with no coals or flame underneath). Spray foil with nonstick cooking spray.

2. Combine tuna, rice, peas, mayonnaise, 1 cup cheese and lemon pepper. Spoon one-fourth of mixture in center of each tortilla. Fold bottom edge of each tortilla up and over filling, just until covered. Fold in opposite sides. Roll up, tucking in sides.

3. Center one tuna wrap, seam side down, on each sheet of foil. Bring up foil sides. Double fold top and ends to seal packet, leaving room for heat circulation inside. Repeat to make four packets.

4. Grill 8 to 10 minutes in covered grill.

5. Sprinkle remaining cheese on top.

Instead of fumbling with those pliers-like pot lifters, pack a pair of insulated leather work gloves, which can be used to handle hot cookware and move burning logs.

Tuscan Stew (Sausage Zuppa)

Best stew your Mama never made.

1 lb ground Italian sausage	**AT CAMP or HOME:** **1.** Sauté sausage and pepper flakes in large pot; drain excess fat; refrigerate.
1½ tsp crushed dry red pepper flakes	
1 lg diced white onion	**2.** In same pan, sauté bacon, onions and garlic over 10w to medium heat until onions are soft (approx. 15 min.).
4 Tbsp bacon pieces	
2 tsp garlic puree	**3.** Add chicken bouillon and water to pot and heat to boil.
10 C. water	
5 cubes chicken buillon	**4.** Add sliced potatoes and cook until soft (approx. 30 min.).
1 C. heavy cream	**5.** Add cream and cook just until heated.
1 lb sliced Russet potatoes (or 3 large other potatoes)	**6.** Stir in sausage mixture; add kale and heat through.
¼ bunch kale – remove membrane and rough chop	**7.** Allow to cool, ladle into gallon freezer bags & freeze.

AT CAMP:
1. Empty freezer bag into pot, heat and enjoy!

Drinking alcohol increases the body's rate of dehydration.

CLASS 1
CLASS 2
CLASS 3
CLASS 4
CLASS 5

Vegetarian Chipotle Chili

When you forget the meat.

1 Tbsp olive oil
½ C. chopped carrots
1 C. chopped red bell pepper
1 C. chopped green bell pepper
1 C. chopped onion
2 tsp minced garlic
1 Tbsp chili powder
1 Tbsp cumin
1 28 oz can Italian style plum tomatoes with juice- chopped
1 15 oz can red kidney beans rinsed and drained
1 15 oz cannellini beans rinsed and drained
1 15 oz black kidney beans rinsed and drained
1-2 Tbsp chopped canned chipotle chilies in adobo sauce
salt and pepper to taste

AT HOME
1. In a large saucepan, heat olive oil over medium heat.
2. Add carrot, bell peppers, onion and garlic, cook until golden brown (about 10 minutes).
3. Add chili powder and cumin and cook, stirring frequently (2 minutes).
4. Add tomatoes, kidney beans, cannellini beans, black beans and chipotle peppers.
5. Heat to boiling. Reduce heat and simmer until vegetables are tender, string occasionally, about 30 minutes.
6. Add water if mixture is very thick.
7. Season with salt and pepper to taste.
8. Allow to cool, ladle into a one gallon freezer bag and freeze.

AT CAMP:
1. Empty freezer bag into pot, heat through. Add water if necessary.

In avalanche country, the most dangerous route to travel is across the middle of a slope.

Wild Jalapeño Mushroom Salmon with Rice

Some people don't like fish, leave them at home.

Minute Rice (use box guide for 4 servings)
1 C. sliced mushrooms
one bunch fresh basil, rough chopped
2 Jalapeños (to taste), finely chopped
4 cloves garlic, minced
½ C. Tbsp olive oil
Salmon (4 servings = 6 to 8 oz portions) frozen
foil to cover salmon at camp

EQUIPMENT:
• Camp stove
• One boiler pot

AT HOME:
1. Slice mushrooms; chop basil and jalapeños and put in ziploc bag.
2. Mince garlic put in bag.
3. Place salmon in ziploc bag.
4. Refrigerate.

AT CAMP:
1. To hot pan with olive oil, add garlic and fry until slightly brown.
2. Add salmon and a dash of olive oil onto top of fish.
3. Add jalapeño, basil and mushrooms.
4. Cook until desired doneness (approx. 3 minutes per side).
5. Remove and place on foil.
6. To same pan, add water (amount according to rice box instructions); boil.
7. Add minute rice; turn off heat and cover 5-7 minutes. Stir, serve and enjoy.

CLASS 1
CLASS 2
CLASS 3
CLASS 4
CLASS 5

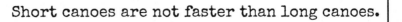

Short canoes are not faster than long canoes.

177

Amy's Backpacking Cinnamon Rolls

Her Sister in law is the baker, she likes to eat them.

Ingredients	Instructions
4 C. flour	**AT CAMP:**
	1. Make "hole" in center of flour.
4 Tbsp dry yeast	
	2. Mix sugar, yeast and water; set aside for few minutes.
warm water (per yeast packet instructions)	
	3. When yeast bubbles, pour into flour hole and mix until it pulls away from sides.
¼ C. butter	
4 Tbsp sugar	**4.** Knead until dough forms; pat with flour; put into gallon ziploc bag; place in warm area to rise to double its size.
2 Tbsp cinnamon	
	5. Roll dough to ½ inch and spread with butter.
	6. Cover with sugar and cinnamon.
	7. Cut into 2" rounds; place into oiled pot.
	8. Cook low and slow until golden; flip and cook other side to golden.

A sewn-in tongue is preferable on a hiking boot.

CLASS 1
CLASS 2
CLASS 3
CLASS 4
CLASS 5

Barbara's Tortilla Soup

The nicest person you will ever meet.

1 lb ground beef

1 (28 oz) can diced tomatoes

1 (16 oz) jar salsa

1 pkg taco seasoning

1 (15 oz) can black beans

1 (12 oz) can tomato sauce

corn chips

AT HOME or CAMP:
1. Brown beef and drain.

2. Add remaining ingredients.

3. Bring to a boil.

4. Simmer for 20 minutes.

5. Top with corn chips.

ENJOY!!!

Never leave home without hard cheese. Pack some aged cheddar, Parmigiano and/or Gruyere (it keeps for at least a week) and you'll come up for new uses for it every day.

Beef Stroganoff

Where's the easy button?

4 oz cooked pasta
⅓ C. cooked ground beef
¼ C crumbled dried mushrooms
2 Tbsp diced dried onion
2 T powdered milk
1 Tbsp flour
1 Tbsp **tomato** powder
1 tsp low sodium beef bouillon
1 tsp powdered **butter**
1 pinch ground black pepper

AT HOME:
1. Pack everything in a quart freezer bag.

AT CAMP:
1. Cover with near boiling water; stir well; seal tightly.

2. Place in a cozy for 15 minutes.

Poison ivy berries are white.

Biscuits and Gravy

Whirled Famous

BISCUITS:
2 C. flour
2 Tbsp sugar
4 tsp baking powder
½ tsp cream of tartar
½ tsp salt
½ C. butter
3 Tbsp buttermilk powder
⅔ C. water (or use canned of milk for richer version)
oil or fat

GRAVY:
Country Gravy Mix 1.25 oz

AT HOME:
1. Combine dry ingredients in quart size freezer Ziploc bag.

AT CAMP:
For biscuits:
1. Heat oil in pan.
2. Add wet ingredients to dry ingredients in Ziploc bag.
3. Knead until dough forms.
4. Flour hands and drop handful size balls into skillet.
5. Cover with lid or foil and cook until brown.

For gravy:
1. Brown sausage in large iron skillet and scrape to one side.
2. Add country gravy mix to 1 cup of water in saucepan.
3. Simmer for 1-2 minutes. Pour over biscuits.

Home dried food tends to have more nutrients too.

Cervidae Finger Steaks

It's an Idaho Thing.

Ingredients	Instructions
1 egg	**AT HOME OR CAMP:**
2 C. buttermilk	**1.** Beat together egg, buttermilk, grill seasoning and ½ C. of flour in large bowl until smooth.
2 Tbsp grill seasoning	**2.** Add beef and toss until well coated.
1½ lbs boneless beef sirloin steak, cut into 2½ x ¼" strips	**3.** Cover with plastic wrap and place into refrigeration to marinate at least 2 hours.
2¼ C. all purpose flour	**4.** Sift 2 C. flour with garlic powder, salt and pepper into large bowl; remove steak strips from batter and allow excess to drain.
2 tsp garlic powder	**5.** Dredge each piece with flour and place onto baking sheet; place into freezer and freeze until firm (1 hr to overnight).
salt and pepper	
3 C. canola oil (for deep frying)	**AT CAMP:** (do not thaw meat) **1.** Heat oil to 370° F (185°C) in deep fryer or cast iron skillet.
plastic wrap	
paper towels	**2.** Drop steak a few pieces at a time into oil and fry until golden; drain on paper towel.

CLASS 1
CLASS 2
CLASS 3
CLASS 4
CLASS 5

In a fast current, the most hazardous wading route is a straight across the current.

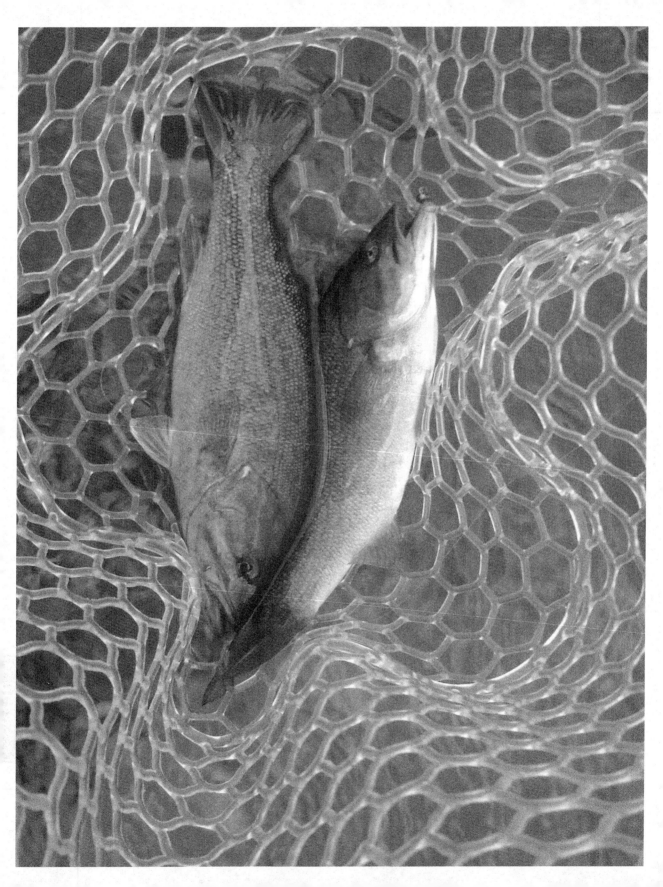

Citrus Grilled Fish

Jimmy Buffets Breakfast

4 fillets of firm fish such as salmon, halibut or cod	**AT HOME:** **1.** Mix ingredients for butter; place in sealable bag for transport to camp.
salt and pepper to taste	**AT CAMP:**
Citrus: limes, lemons, oranges	**1.** Preheat grill to medium-low heat; clean and lightly oil grill.
4 squares of foil	
	2. Season fish with salt and pepper.
Citrus Herb Butter:	**3.** Cut lemons, limes and oranges into large slices; arrange on cooler side of grill.
1 stick unsalted butter, softened	
½ tsp grated orange zest	**4.** Top fruit and fish with fresh herbs.
2 tsp fresh orange juice	**5.** Dab all with butter.
¼ tsp cayenne pepper	**6.** Cover with foil and cook until fish is opaque in center (no need to turn), approx. 20-30 min.
1 clove garlic, minced	
2 Tbsp chopped herbs*	
½ tsp coarse salt	
*Fresh herb options: Cilantro, basil, mint or parsley	

The storm is 2 miles away when you see a flash of lightning and count to ten before hearing thunder.

Cole's Chicken Fajitas

The Fajita expert and a fine Brother in law.

2 Tbsp vegetable oil
1 lb boneless skinless chicken breasts (or beef sirloin steak) cut into ¼ inch strips
1 medium onion, cut into thin strips
1 medium bell pepper (green or red or combination of both), cut into thin strips
¼ C. water
1 pkg McCormick® Fajita Seasoning Mix
8 – 6 in. flour tortillas

TOPPINGS:
· salsa
· sour cream
· guacamole
· shredded cheese
· chopped tomatoes

AT HOME:
1. Prepare chicken and vegetables and put into freezer bags; put tortillas into foil and insert into ziplock bag.

AT CAMP:
1. Remove tortillas from baggie; gently warm.

2. Heat 1 Tbsp of the oil in large skillet on medium high heat.

3. Add chicken; cook and stir 3 minutes until no longer pink; remove from skillet.

4. Heat remaining 1 Tbsp of oil in same skillet; add onion and bell pepper; cook and stir 3-5 minutes.

5. Return chicken to skillet; stir in water and seasoning mix.

6. Cook 3 minutes or until heated through.

7. Spoon chicken onto tortillas; add toppings.

Clothing that is too tight will not actually keep you warmer in the cold.

Dad's Cioppino

Hey Dad, thank you for my culinary passion!

¼ C. olive oil
1 medium green bell pepper, seeded and chopped
1¼ C. chopped onion
1 – 28 oz can each: Italian plum tomatoes with basil
2 Tbsp tomato paste
2 C. dry red wine
1¼ tsp each: dried basil; dried thyme and dried oregano
⅛ tsp salt
1 bay leaf
2 Tbsp hot pepper flakes
1 sprig fresh parsley
24 hard shell clams, scrubbed
¼ lbs shrimp, peeled and deveined; tail on
1-2 lbs halibut or other firm white fish, cut into cubes
¼ lbs sea scallops, halved
1 Tbsp chopped parsley

AT HOME:
1. Heat olive oil in 4 qt saucepan with lid over medium heat; add pepper and onion; cook until soft; stirring frequently.

2. Add tomatoes, wine and herbs; heat to boiling; reduce and simmer 1¼ hours, stirring and scraping bottom of pan occasionally.

3. Discard bay leaf and parsley sprig.

4. Heat to full boil; add clams; cover; check every 5 min to total of 20 min, removing clams that have opened; discard any unopened clams after 20 min.

5. Season with salt to taste; add remaining seafood; simmer 5-7 min. or until white fish is flaky; stir in clams.

6. Sprinkle with chopped parsley; cool and place into 1 gallon freezer bag.

AT CAMP:
1. Heat and serve with crusty french bread (optional).

Use leftover/broken graham crackers and chocolate to make inside-out s'mores: Melt chocolate in a cup, warm a marshmallow over the fire, then dip it in chocolate and roll it in crushed graham crackers. Eat it right off the stick.

Easy, Cheesy
Southern Jambalaya

Put some South in your Mouth!

1 pouch Knorr-Lipton Cajun Sides Red Beans & Rice	**AT HOME:** **1.** Pack fresh veggies in paper bags or sealable plastic container. **2.** Put dry ingredients into sealable snack bag.
1 - 4 oz pouch southwest flavored chicken breast	
1 packet Jack Link's JackPack! cheese-sausage-pretzel	**AT CAMP:** **1.** If using dehydrated, rehydrate veggies. **2.** Dice JackPack! sausage and cheese. **3.** Chop chicken.
1 Tbsp chopped onion or green onion or 1 tsp dried onion flakes	**4.** Sauté vegetables and sausage chunks in oil until tender. **5.** Add water; bring to boil. **6.** Add chicken and beans and rice package.
2 Tbsp diced red bell pepper	**7.** Simmer, covered 8 min.
2 Tbsp diced celery or 2 tsp dried	**8.** Sprinkle with cheese.
1 Tbsp olive oil	**9.** Remove from heat and let stand, covered 3 minutes.
2 C. water	

CLASS 1
CLASS 2
CLASS 3
CLASS 4
CLASS 5

While you hike, soak lentils in an extra water bottle (2 cups water to 1 cup lentils). At the end of the day, simmer until tender (it only takes a few minutes), then use in soups, salads, wraps, etc.

Fadgen's French Onion Noodle Bowl

The dad and the son, the son might be famous some day.

3 oz pkg ramen noodles (baked is best); discard flavor packet

3 Tbsp diced dried onion

2 T cooked and dehydrated ground beef (or vegetarian beef product)

2 Tbsp low sodium beef bouillon

1 Tbsp celery flakes

¼ tsp ground black pepper

¼ C. instant stuffing mix

2 C. water

AT HOME:
1. Pack onion, beef, bouillon, celery and pepper in a small bag.

2. Pack stuffing mix in separate bag and tuck in noodles.

AT CAMP:
1. To water, add 1st bag ingredients.

2. Let sit 5-10 minutes to soak.

3. Bring to boil; add ramen and cook 3 min.

4. Remove from heat and top with stuffing mix.

5. Simmer, covered 8 min.

6. Sprinkle with cheese.

7. Remove from heat and let stand, covered 3 minutes.

The first symptom of frostbite is numbness.

Franklin's Alpine Fish Fry

A good friend and a not so good fisherman.

2 Tbsp olive oil
½ onion minced
2 garlic cloves, minced
¼ C. white wine
1 can (8oz) diced tomatoes
1 tsp salt
¼ C. Kalamata pitted olives, chopped
3 tsp capers
1 tsp red pepper flakes (optional)
4 fish fillets – halibut or other firm fish
¼ C. fresh parsley, chopped
pepper to taste

AT CAMP:

1. Heat oil in skillet over medium heat; add shallots and sauté three minutes.

2. Add garlic and sauté 1 minute.

3. Add wine and reduce by half.

4. Add tomatoes and salt; heat through (about 2 min.).

5. Add olives, capers and pepper flakes; add black pepper to taste; cook 5 min.

6. Nestle fish into sauce without overlapping.

7. Spoon sauce over fish.

8. Cook 6-8 min. or until fish is flaky and pulls apart easily when pierced with a fork.

9. Remove pan from heat; stir in parsley and serve.

The approach of high winds is indicated by clouds tinged with red that float high at sunset.

Fried Camp Pies

If only you could pack ice cream.

1 can (8oz) favorite fruit pie filling

1 C. large refrigerator biscuits

margarine or butter

cinnamon sugar

paper towels

AT CAMP:

1. Roll out one biscuit.

2. Place large spoonful of filling in center.

3. Fold over and crimp edges.

4. Fry in butter or margarine on low to medium heat until golden brown.

5. Sprinkle with cinnamon sugar as soon as removed from heat.

EAT CAREFULLY AS FILLINGS GET HOT !!

GORP stands for Good Old Raisins and Peanuts, a quick energy trail snack.

Boundary

TRAIL NO. 245

⬆ JCT E FK PINE CR TR NO 263 3
⬆ JCT BIG FLAT TR NO 352   7
⬆ JCT RUSH CR TR NO 262   9

Fry Bread

A Squaw Butte Classic

Ingredients	Instructions
1 C. all purpose flour	**AT CAMP:** 1. Mix all ingredients.
1½ tsp baking powder	2. Add water.
¼ tsp salt	3. Mix quickly to capture release of the powder.
½ C. water	4. Heat oil in large skillet or fryer.
Cooking oil (enough to fry dough without it touching bottom of pan)	5. Form dough into bun shape and drop into pan. 6. Fry 5 minutes on each side until golden brown.
paper towels	7. Test with toothpick for doneness.
* Cinnamon/Sugar or Honey Butter	8. Drain on paper towel.

A frostbitten area should NEVER be rubbed.

George's Clam Chowder

He took it from a little old lady from Boston.

CLASS 1

CLASS 2

CLASS 3

CLASS 4

CLASS 5

6 – 8 medium
baker potatoes
1 large onion
4 large garlic
cloves, chopped
1 can cream of
celery soup
1 pint half and
half
2 C. water
3 – 6.5 oz cans
chopped clams
with juice
1 "glug" sherry
Salt and pepper
to taste
6 shakes (or more
or less to taste)
tabasco
1 C. fresh celery,
chopped
1 lb. bacon

AT CAMP:

1. Chop bacon and fry until crisp.

2. Remove bacon to paper towel.

3. To bacon grease, add potatoes, onions, celery and garlic.

4. Add remaining ingredients except ½ and ½ and bacon.

5. Cook until potatoes are soft.

6. Add bacon and ½ and ½.

7. Simmer to blend.

If you are attacked by a bear, you should play dead, curl in a ball and lock your hands behind your head.

Herbed Tomato Rice

Goes great with fresh caught fish.

1 C. instant rice

¼ C. freeze-dried corn

¼ C. sun-dried tomatoes

1 Tbsp diced dried onion

1½ tsp lower sodium beef or chicken bouillon

1 tsp granulated garlic

¼ tsp dried oregano

1 Tbsp or one packet olive oil

2 oz cheddar, co-jack or pepper-jack cheese, diced

1¼ C. water

AT HOME:
1. Pack the rice and oregano into a quart freezer bag.

2. Tuck in packets of oil and cheese.

AT CAMP:
1. Bring water to boil.

2. Add oil and dry ingredients.

3. Remove from heat and cover tightly for 15 min.

4. Fold in diced cheese.

The word camouflage is actually derived from the French word camoufler, meaning "to blind or veil."

Chocolate French Toast

This is best used when taking a date camping...sort of makes up a bit for the lack of modern conveniences.

4 eggs
⅔ C. milk
1 packet hot chocolate mix
8 thick slices 2 day old bread
2 Tbsp butter or oil

CONDIMENTS:
• butter
• chocolate syrup

AT CAMP:

1. In shallow bowl, beat eggs, milk and hot chocolate mix.

2. Dip each slice of bread into mixture, allowing bread to soak up the liquid.

3. In large skillet over medium heat, melt butter or vegetable oil.

4. Add bread pieces; fry until brown on both sides.

5. Serve hot with butter and chocolate syrup.

The primary reason that our feathered friends migrate South in the Fall, or North in the Spring, does not solely lie in the cold of winter, as most are well-equipped to survive in extreme temperatures, but instead lies with the upcoming shortage of food.

Spaghetti Carbonara

Truly, pasta is one of the greatest gifts to campers.

8 oz spaghetti pasta, broken into thirds
1 Tbsp olive oil (or one packet)
¼ C. onions, chopped
3 Tbsp minced garlic
2 eggs, beaten
1 packet lemon juice
¼ C. seasoned bread crumbs
¼ C. shelf stable parmesan cheese
1 tsp dried parsley
¼ tsp ground black pepper
4 C. water

AT HOME:
1. Pack spaghetti into sandwich bag.

2. Place breadcrumbs, cheese, parsley and pepper into snack bag.

3. Carry everything else in separate snack bags.

AT CAMP:
1. Bring water to boil.

2. Add pasta and cook for time on pkg; drain, reserving ¼ cup of the water.

3. Add oil, onions, garlic, lemon juice, eggs and reserved water to the pot.

4. Toss to combine.

5. Sprinkle with breadcrumbs and toss to combine. Using a wide fry pan lid.

The best coffee for camping is Starbucks Via packets, which produce café-quality caffeine with no waste and no bulky beans or equipment.

PEELABLE SEAL ↑

Meal, Ready-to-Eat,
Individual

Recommended,
ghter Tested,
ter Approved™

MRE™

14

MENU 14
RATATOUILLE
VEGETARIAN

THE WORNICK COMPANY
CINCINNATI, OHIO 45242

U.S. GOVERNMENT PROPERTY
COMMERCIAL RESALE IS UNLAWFUL

ATION HEATERS ARE PROHIBITED ON COMMERC
UNLESS SEALED IN ORIGINAL MRE MENU BAG

Margo's Ratatouille

She don't do gluten, and she doesn't do the stuff in the bag to the left.

1 eggplant, diced
4 tsp olive oil
2 onions, diced
1 red and 1 yel-
low pepper, diced
2 garlic cloves,
smashed
1 tsp fennel seed
2 bay leaves
1 tsp Herbes de
Provence or dried
thyme
2 small zucchini,
diced
2 C. fresh
tomatoes or
1 14.5 oz can
diced tomatoes
salt and pepper
(to taste)

NOTE:
Herbs de Provence
can be found in
the spice section
of most grocery
stores and typi-
cally contains
rosemary, marjo-
ram, basil, bay
leaf, and thyme.

AT HOME:
1. Peel eggplant and cut into diagonal ½" slices.
2. Squeeze eggplant between paper towels to remove excess liquid.
3. Dice eggplant and other vegetables into small pieces. (If planning to dehydrate the meal, cut into larger pieces.)
4. In large, non-stick skillet, heat oil and sauté onions until translucent.
5. Add garlic, peppers, fennel, bay leaves and Herbs or thyme; sauté until soft.
6. Add eggplant and sauté until golden.
7. Add zucchini and sauté 5 min.
8. Add tomatoes, salt and pepper; simmer 15 min.
9. Cool and place into 1 gal. freezer bag; let sit overnight; freeze for trail.

AT CAMP:
1. Re-heat.

Grizzly, black bears, hummingbirds and squirrels hibernate in the winter because a long, chilly season of little food and warmth is no picnic for these animals.

Borah
CAMPGROUND

CHALLIS
National Forest

• US DEPARTMENT OF AGRICULTURE •

Mt. Borah Baggie Omelet

Can be cooked on Chicken Out Ridge. Named for the tallest mountain in Idaho, which is saying a lot.

Eggs (1-2 per person)
1 Tbsp Milk per egg

any or all of the following:
cheese, ham, bacon(cooked and crumbled), onions, peppers, tomatoes mushrooms

pita bread, bagel or English muffin

Ziploc freezer bag

4 C. water

AT CAMP:

1. Chop ingredients.

2. Put 1-2 eggs into a baggie and add desired amount of milk.

3. Add additional ingredients.

4. Seal bag tightly.

5. Place bag into boiling water and cook 3-5 minutes until desired doneness.

6. To serve as breakfast sandwich, place omelet onto bagel, English muffin or pita bread.

Deer shed their antlers annually as a prelude to the regeneration, or re-growth, of new ones.

CLASS 1

CLASS 2

CLASS 3

CLASS 4

CLASS 5

Pettit Lake Backpacker Pizza

A pizza on a backpacking stove? Really?

3 C. of Original Bisquick Mix

⅔ C. very hot water

2 Tbsp olive oil

1 8 oz can of pizza sauce

1 Pkg (¼ oz) sliced pepperoni

¼ C. of sliced mushrooms

1½ C. shredded mozzarella

AT HOME
1. Put Bisquick in a ziploc plastic bag.
2. Put sliced mushrooms put in a ziploc bag.
3. Put mozzarella in a ziploc bag.

AT CAMP:
1. Mix Bisquick, olive oil and hot water in a bowl, mix and cover with a towel for 8 minutes.
2. Form into ball and place dough onto a flat surface
3. Divide in 4, and shape each piece into a 6-inch round.
4. Fire up the stove; use the fry pan for the bottom and the bottom of the 1-2 litter pot for the top creating and oven.
5. Put a tablespoon of olive oil in the fry pan, place 6 inch round dough in fry pan and put the pot on top.
6. Keep the heat real low (simmer), bake for 1 minute, cut heat completely check and flip if necessary.
7. Repeat 1 more minute if necessary.
8. Flip, add cheese, meat and mushrooms, and cook for another 1 minute keeping the pot on top. Turn heat completely off and let stand inside the hooded pot for 5 minutes.
9. Repeat 3 more times alternating toppings if desired.

Olives, pickled vegetables, oil-marinated tomatoes, peppers and onions, and bocconcini all make great mix-ins for cooked grains and pasta--and are great for snacking on their own.

Ramen and Summer Sausage

A knife, boiling water and Ta Da.

1 pkg beef ramen noodles

2 C. water

summer sausage

NOTE:
Summer sausage can be a heavy food item to carry so plan recipes to use at beginning of trip.

AT CAMP:

1. Make ramen noodles according to package instructions.

2. Cut up chunks of summer sausage and mix into noodles.

More species of fish live in a single tributary of the Amazon River than in all the rivers in North America combined.

Red Bean Stew

Warms your cockles, and a warm cockle is a good thing.

¼ C. dried diced carrot

¼ C. crumbled dried mushrooms

¼ C. diced sun-dried tomatoes

1 can red kidney beans

4 oz cooked and small shaped pasta

1 tsp low sodium beef (or vegetable) bouillon

¼ tsp dried garlic

¼ tsp ground black pepper

2 Tsp shelf stable parmesan cheese

AT HOME:
1. Pack everything into quart freezer bag.

AT CAMP:
1. Add near boiling water to cover dry items.

2. Stir well; seal tightly.

3. Put into cozy for 15 minutes.

The most carnivorous of all bears is the polar bear. Its diet consists almost entirely of seals and fish.

Spicy Meatball Burritos

This was inspired after a Pacific Crest Jaunt.

SAUCE:
1 lb (large can) diced tomatoes
1 large jalapeño pepper, chopped
1 clove garlic, minced
1 Tbsp chili powder
1 tsp dried oregano
1 tsp sugar
½ tsp salt
¼ C. sliced ripe olives

MEATBALLS:
1½ lb hamburger
½ C. chopped parsley
½ C. minced onion
1 egg
3 Tbsp parmesan cheese
1 tsp ground cumin
½ tsp salt
¼ tsp pepper

Serve on flour tortillas
Toppings: Sour cream and shredded cheese

AT HOME:
Sauce:
1. In a large saucepan, combine all sauce ingredients; simmer on low heat while making meatballs (15-30 min.).

Meatballs:
1. Preheat oven to 500°.

2. Mix meatball ingredients then roll into 1" balls.

3. Place onto baking sheet (close together) and bake 7 minutes or until no longer pink inside.

4. Place meatballs into sauce.

5. Cool; put into freezer bag.

6. Serve in over tortillas; add toppings.

AT CAMP:
1. 1. Reheat and roll into tortillas; add toppings.

The mudskipper is a fish that can actually walk on land.

Super Dave Donuts

If this was all that you made, Super Dave would be just fine.

2 cans refrigerator biscuits	**AT CAMP:** **1.** Place oil in skillet.
2 C. hot oil	**2.** Open cans of biscuits and separate each; poke hole in middles.
1 C. powdered sugar	**3.** Place in hot oil and flip when brown, using wooden tongs.
OR	**4.** Remove from oil and drain on paper towel.
1 C. sugar with 1 – 2 Tbsp cinnamon	**5.** While still warm place into powdered or cinnamon sugar.
paper towels	

You pretty much can't get away from bacon or whiskey in the South. Put a doughnut in it and you'd be good to go.
Hillary Scott

CLASS 1
CLASS 2
CLASS 3
CLASS 4
CLASS 5

The 45 Liter Backpack Burrito

Closely resembling a local favorite.

4 large flour

Burrito size tortillas

1 lb of fried new potatoes (Baby Red or Gold's)

1 lb breakfast sausage

4 eggs

1 bunch cilantro

2 C. pepper jack cheese

1 C. of salsa

1 can black beans (drained)

AT HOME:

1. Fry sausage in frying pan, remove sausage and put in a bowl.

2. Add potatoes with the grease still in the pan fry the potatoes to the level you desire.

3. Scramble the eggs in with the potatoes.

4. Add sausage back in and Black Beans if desired, layout the portion you desire on the tortilla.

5. Then add the cilantro, cheese and salsa.

6. Roll up burrito and wrap in heavy duty foil- refrigerate the night before and take with you in your backpack for a breakfast, trail or summit lunch.

Most fish eggs are almost yolkless, since they are laid in water where food for the unborn fish is readily available.

White Bean Chicken Chili

Perfect for feeding six hungry Boy Scouts, or twelve hungry normal folks.

2 Tbsp olive oil
1 medium onion, chopped
2 fresh jalapeño, deveined, seeded and chopped (leave vein and seeds for hotter chili)
4 cloves garlic, minced
2 lbs ground chicken or boneless breast cut into very small pieces
1 Tbsp oregano
1 Tbsp chili powder
2 Tbsp cumin
3 Tbsp flour
3 - 15 oz cans northern white beans, drained and rinsed
4 C. chicken broth
1½ C. frozen corn
1 bunch Swiss chard or kale, stems removed, chopped
¼ tsp crushed red pepper flakes
salt and pepper to taste
¼ C. chopped Italian parsley or cilantro

AT HOME:
1. In large heavy bottom saucepan, heat oil over medium heat.
2. Add onion and cook until translucent (5 min); add garlic and jalapeño.
3. Add chicken and spices; cook until chicken is cooked through (approx. 8 min.); stir in flour.
4. Add beans, chard or kale, corn and chicken stock; scrape bottom to retrieve brown bits.
5. Simmer 55-60 min. until liquid reduced by half.
6. Add pepper flakes; stir and cook 10 min.
7. Season with salt and pepper (to taste).
8. Cool; ladle into 1 gallon freezer bag; freeze.

AT CAMP:
1. Place into pot and bring to boil.
2. Simmer 2 minutes.

"Whenever I meet someone who does not consider chili a favorite dish, then I've usually found someone who has never tasted good chili." - Jan Butel

Babi Ketjap

Expedition to Carstensz Pyramid (4,884 m) is one of the most exotic mountaineering trips imaginable. It is considered the highest peak of the seventh continent (Australia/Oceania) for climbers attempting the Seven Summits. Most of the climbers call it Carstensz Pyramid after Jan Carstensz, a Dutch explorer, who was the first European to sight the peak of the mountain in the 1623. In 1962, Heinrich Harrier became the first foreigner to reach the summit of this peak.

1 lb pork tenderloin
1 large onion
2 cloves garlic
3 Tbsp fresh ground ginger
¼ C. brown sugar
½ C. Kecap Manis (sweet Indonesian soy sauce) or other soy sauce
2 C. water
2 Tbsp. lemon juice
1 cube pork bouillon
salt and pepper to taste

AT HOME:

1. Finely dice onion, garlic and ginger and place into separate sealable bags.

2. Cut pork into strips; place into sealable bag.

AT CAMP:

1. Add onion, garlic and ginger to fry pan.

2. Add pork and cook until onion is soft and pork is dark.

3. Add soy sauce, water, lemon juice and bouillon.

4. Simmer on low for approx. 30 minutes.

5. Serve with boiled or fried rice.

"Carstensz Pyramid would be by far the most technical mountain I would have ever climbed."
Jordon Romero, youngest Seven Summits climber

Bliny (Russian Pancakes) and Filling

Mount Elbrus, the highest mountain in Europe, one of the Seven Summits, and one of the most popular but deadliest high mountains in the world.

3 eggs	**AT CAMP:**
2 Tbsp sugar	**1.** Beat eggs until foamy.
½ tsp salt	**2.** Add sugar, salt and milk.
1¼ C. milk	**3.** Add flour and mix until there are no lumps; add vanilla.
1 cup flour (buckwheat is traditional)	**4.** Pour oil into pan; when hot, pour thin layer of mixture into pan.
½ tsp vanilla	**5.** Cook until edges turn light brown; flip to cook other side.
2 Tbsp vegetable oil	**6.** Serve with filling or fruit, butter, jam, sour cream.
BLINY FILLING:	
1 pkg frozen berries	FILLING:
¼ C. water	**1.** Thaw berries; place into saucepan.
2 Tbsp cornstarch	**2.** Dissolve cornstarch in water.
	3. Cook on slow heat until thickened.

"You never climb the same mountain twice, not even in memory. Memory rebuilds the mountain, changes the weather, retells the jokes, remakes all the moves."
Lito Tejada-Flores

Damien's Chili Salmon Taters

The highest point in all Antarctica is Vinson Massif, now famous as one of the "Seven Summits". Sometimes referred to as "Mount Vinson", it is named after a U.S. congressman from Georgia.

2 Tbsp powdered milk
⅓ C. water + ¾ C. water
1 C. dehydrated mashed potatoes
½ tsp salt
¼ tsp black pepper
1 Tbsp butter
1 – 7 oz foil pack of smoked salmon
2 Tbsp chili powder

AT CAMP:

1. Mix all ingredients except butter in a bowl.

2. Form into patties.

3. Add butter to skillet and heat on medium.

4. Add patties and cook until brown (about 4-6 minutes.

"Somewhere between the bottom of the climb and the summit is the answer to the mystery why we climb."
Greg Child

Denali Salmon Quesadillas with Chipotle Mayonnaise

Mount McKinley, or Denali (Koyukon Athabaskan for "The High One", Dghelaayce'e in Ahtna), in Alaska, is the highest mountain peak in the United States.

1 foil pack (6 oz) salmon Chicken of the Sea, skinless and boneless
4- 10" whole wheat tortillas
2 tsp olive oil
¾ C. shredded cheddar
¼ C. Monterey jack cheese
2 C. canned black beans, rinsed

CHIPOTLE MAYONNAISE:
¼ C. mayonnaise
¼ C. chopped roasted peppers
1 chipotle chile in adobo sauce
1 Tbsp barbecue sauce
1 tsp minced garlic
¼ tsp salt
¼ tsp black pepper

AT HOME:

1. Place all mayonnaise ingredients into food processor and blend until smooth.

2. Put into sealable container.

AT CAMP:

1. Place tortilla into pan coated with olive oil.

2. Top with ¼ of the cheese, beans and salmon.

3. Drizzle with mayonnaise.

4. Cook 2-3 minutes until bottom is brown and cheese is melted.

5. Fold in half; repeat for remaining tortillas.

6. Cut into half and serve warm.

"Remember that time spent on a rock climb isn't subtracted from your life span."
—Will Niccolls

Papas Fritas Con Rajas

Aconcagua is the highest peak in both the Western and Southern Hemispheres. It is one of the Seven Summits.

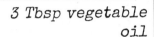

3 Tbsp vegetable oil	**AT HOME:**
	1. Cut onions into ¼" pieces; place into sealable bag.
1 medium white onion	2. Devein peppers and cut lengthwise into ¼" strips; place into sealable bag.
2 lbs red potatoes, scrubbed	**AT CAMP:**
	1. Heat skillet on medium heat; add oil and onion; cook until soft (about 2-3 minutes).
¼ tsp salt	
¼ tsp black pepper	2. Cut potatoes into ¼" slices; add to skillet with salt and pepper; toss until potatoes start to brown (about 8-10 minutes).
2 large poblano peppers	
	3. Add pepper strips and reduce heat to medium low.
	4. Cover and cook approx. 7-10 minutes until potatoes are tender and brown.

"In the mountains there are only two grades: You can either do it, or you can't."
—Rusty Baille

Pilau Rice

Kilimanjaro, with its three volcanic cones, Kibo, Mawenzi, and Shira, is a dormant volcano in Kilimanjaro National Park, Tanzania and the highest mountain in Africa.

1½ Tbsp cumin
1 Tbsp cardamom
⅛ tsp black pepper
½ tsp cinnamon
¼ tsp cloves
1 C. raw rice
2 C. cold water
⅛ large onion, diced
⅛ large green (or red) pepper, diced
⅛ large carrot, diced
⅛ C. diced celery
2 cloves minced garlic
1 Tbsp olive oil

AT HOME:

1. Mix spices and put into sealable bag.

2. Place rice in sealable bag.

3. Place vegetables and garlic in sealable bag.

4. Put oil into non-spill container.

AT CAMP:

1. In 2 liter pot, put water and rice.

2. Add 1 Tbsp of spice and bring to boil; stir and simmer covered approx. 20 minutes.

3. Put oil into fry pan and add vegetables and garlic; cook until tender.

4. Add to rice and stir until all liquid is absorbed.

"On this proud and beautiful mountain we have lived hours of fraternal, warm and exalting nobility. Here for a few days we have ceased to be slaves and have really been men. It is hard to return to servitude."
Lionel Terray

Tsampa

Simply, the highest mountain on Earth.

¼ C. water or soy milk	**AT CAMP:** **1.** Boil liquid then pour into bowl.
1 Tbsp margarine	**2.** Add margarine and stir.
½ C. roasted barley flour	**3.** Add flour and mix by hand until dough forms.
salt and sugar to taste	**4.** Add sugar.
	5. Add flour and mix until there are no lumps.
	6. Add vanilla.

* Tsampa is quite simple to prepare; indeed, it is known as a convenience food and often used by sherpas, nomads, and other travelers. While traditional tsampa is prepared with tea, water or beer are sometimes used in its place. It may also be prepared as porridge.

"Many years ago, I climbed the mountains, even thought it is forbidden. Things are not as they teach us; the world is hollow, and I have touched the sky."
Gene Roddenberry

Index O' Recipes

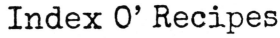

In The Wild Chef

"I should have no objection to go over the same life from its beginning to the end: requesting only the advantage authors have, of correcting in a second edition the faults of the first."
Benjamin Franklin

Stephen Weston is a rabid outdoor enthusiast living in Boise, Idaho. Steve learned his cooking craft early growing up in Oregon, working in restaurants and seeing his stepfather RL pamper his mother. A favorite camping companion of many at Idahosummits.com, he has contributed to the fattening of waistlines across North America. During his Army years in Europe and West Germany, Steve honed his culinary skills, taking his love of cooking from a hobby to proficiency. He is supported in his culinary adventures around the globe by his lovely wife Amy and his daughter Chelsea, and sons Tanner and Slade. This is his first book, but definitely not the last.

In The Wild Chef is often times referred to as a backpacking gourmet snob cookbook. The Author has thought of everything from Curry dishes to Italian desserts in the backcountry. Breaking down the recipes in classes like are used in Hiking and Mountaineering! Class 1 being the easiest and as you progress to Class 5 you are cooking from scratch.

"Eat well outdoors"